ENCOUNTERING
CHUPACABRA
AND OTHER CRYPTIDS
EYEWITNESS ACCOUNTS

by Megan Cooley Peterson

illustrated by Matthew Stevens

Consultant:
Jerome Clark
J. Allen Hynek Center for UFO Studies
Chicago, Illinois

CAPSTONE PRESS
a capstone imprint

ISBN 978-1-4914-0242-9 (library binding)
ISBN 978-1-4914-0247-4 (ebook PDF)

Speech and thought bubbles in red are direct quotations from eyewitness accounts.

Design Elements
Shutterstock: alanadesign, Mika Shysh

Designer
Ted Williams

Production Specialist
Laura Manthe

Art Director
Nathan Gassman

Editor
Mandy Robbins

Printed in the United States of America in Stevens Point, Wisconsin.
032014   008092WZF14

TABLE OF CONTENTS

*Stories in this book are taken from eyewitness
accounts and cannot be proven true or false.

A BLOODTHIRSTY CRYPTID

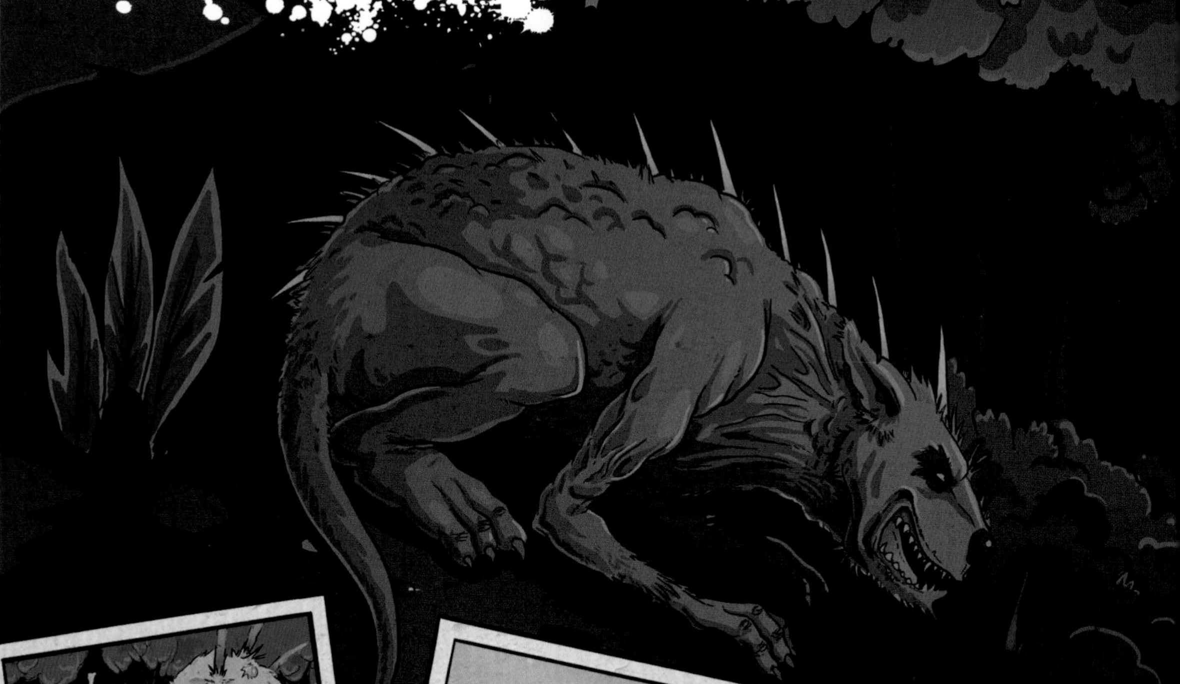

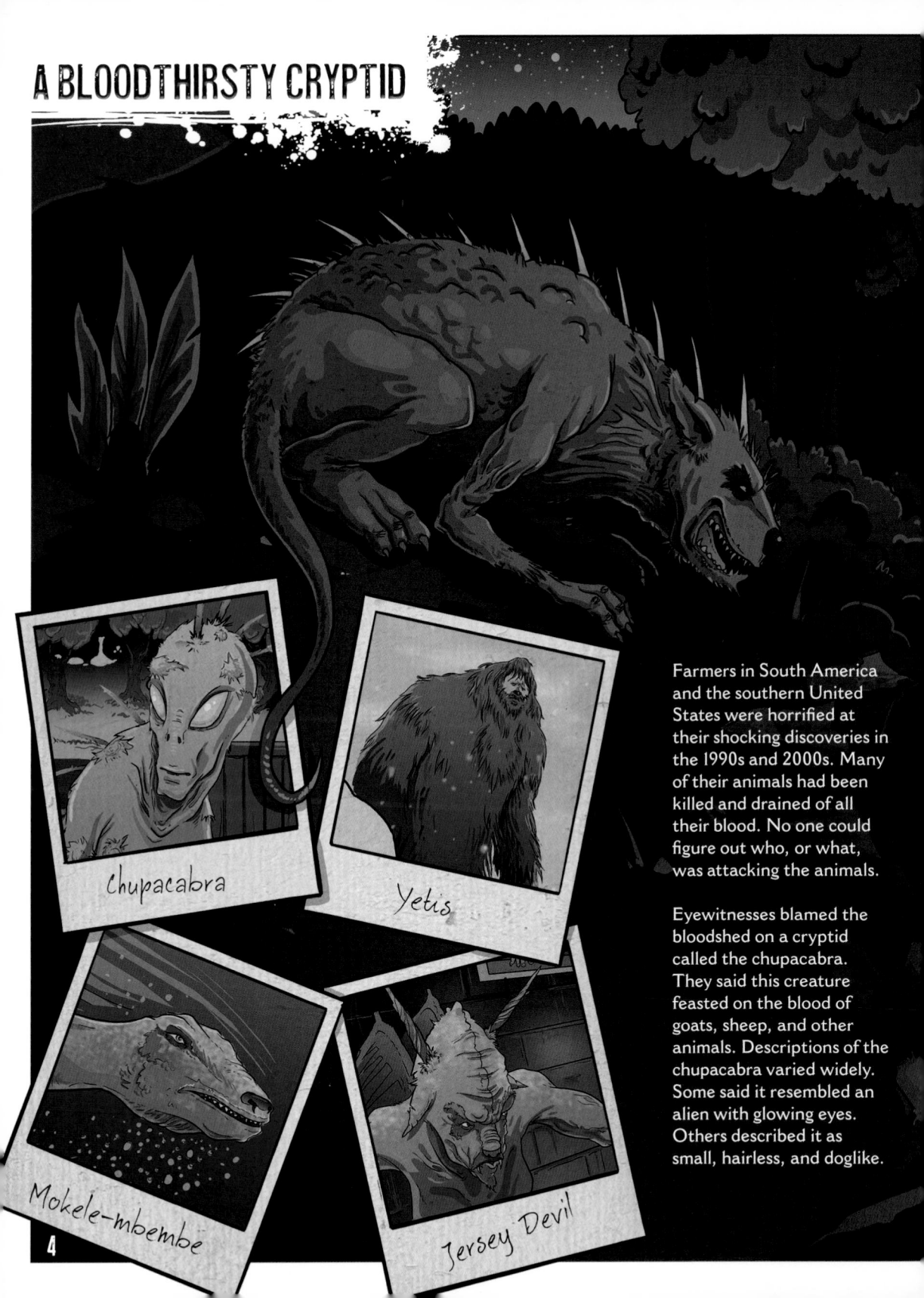

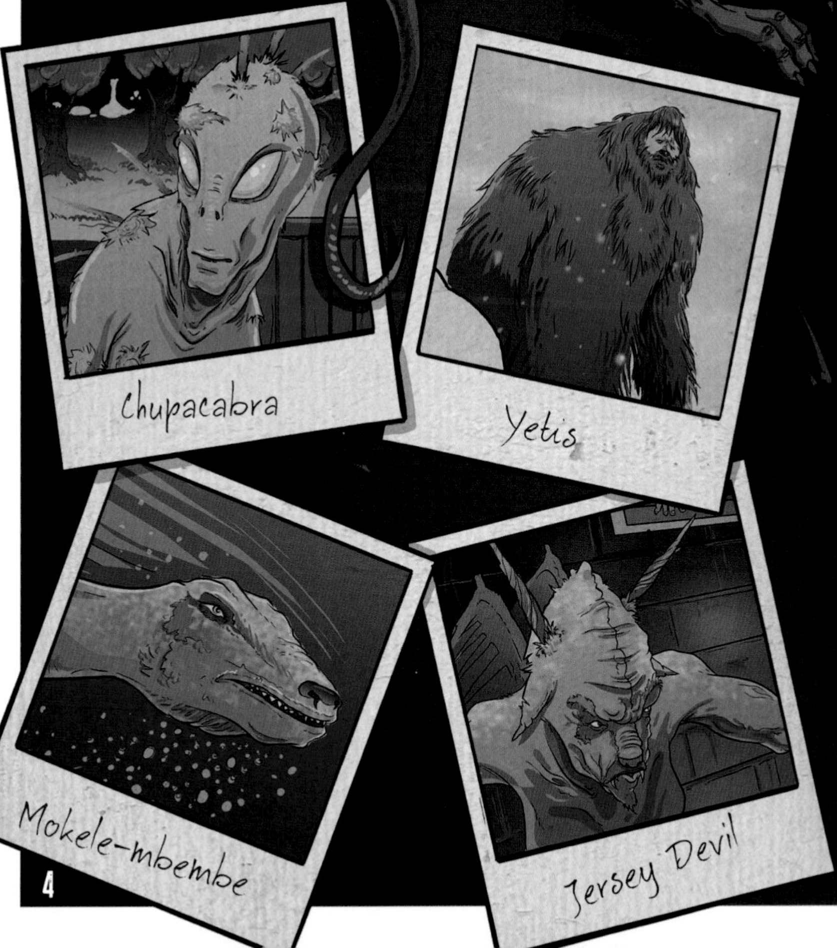
Chupacabra
Yetis
Mokele-mbembe
Jersey Devil

Farmers in South America and the southern United States were horrified at their shocking discoveries in the 1990s and 2000s. Many of their animals had been killed and drained of all their blood. No one could figure out who, or what, was attacking the animals.

Eyewitnesses blamed the bloodshed on a cryptid called the chupacabra. They said this creature feasted on the blood of goats, sheep, and other animals. Descriptions of the chupacabra varied widely. Some said it resembled an alien with glowing eyes. Others described it as small, hairless, and doglike.

Although chupacabra sightings have happened only recently, cryptids have been reported for hundreds of years. The existence of legendary, unproven creatures remains a mystery. But a few cryptids have been proven to be real animals. The giant squid was once thought to be a monster called the Kraken. Are other cryptids crafty enough to stay hidden? Or are they simply the stuff of scary campfire tales?

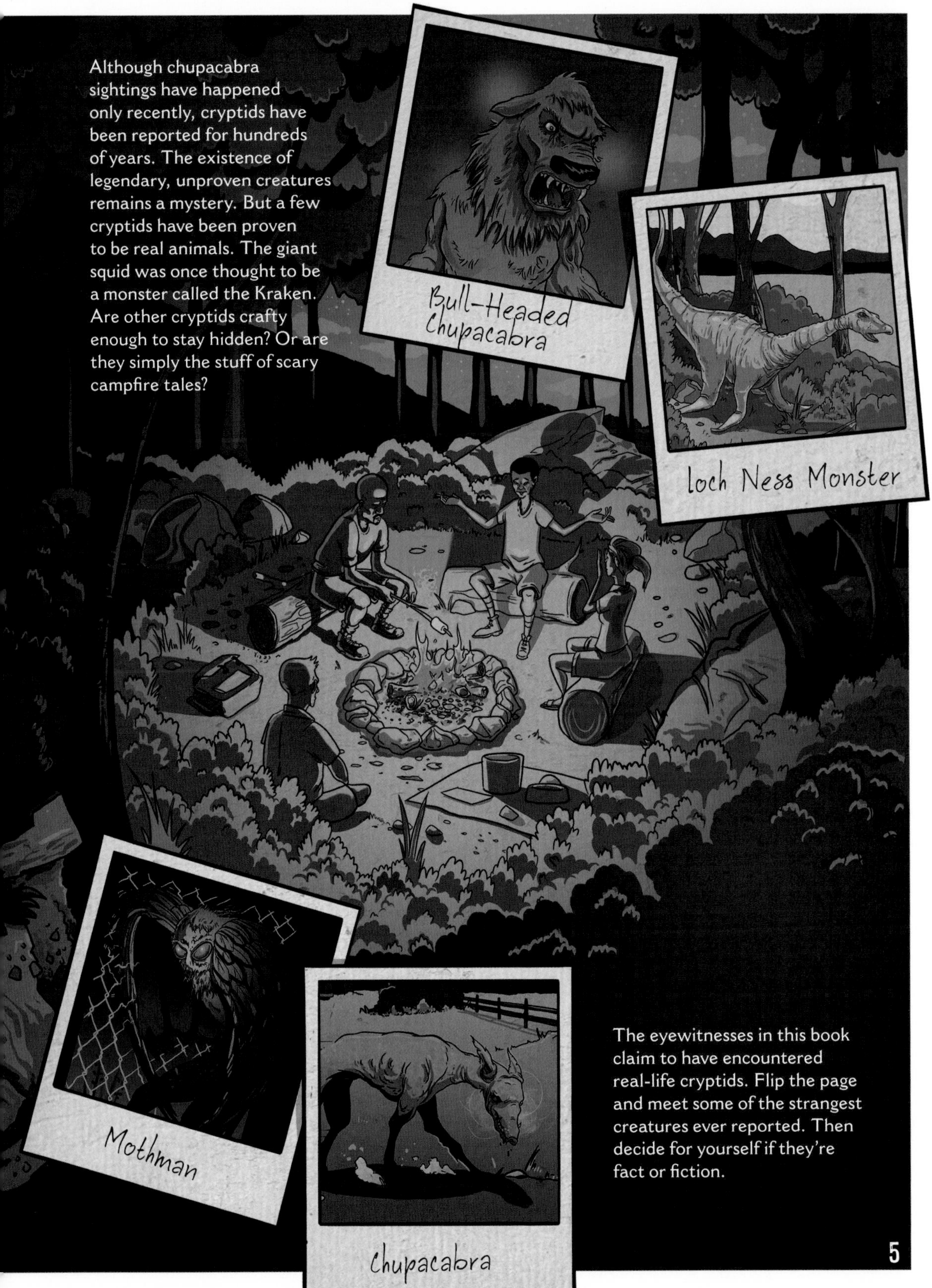
Bull-Headed Chupacabra
loch Ness Monster
Mothman
Chupacabra

The eyewitnesses in this book claim to have encountered real-life cryptids. Flip the page and meet some of the strangest creatures ever reported. Then decide for yourself if they're fact or fiction.

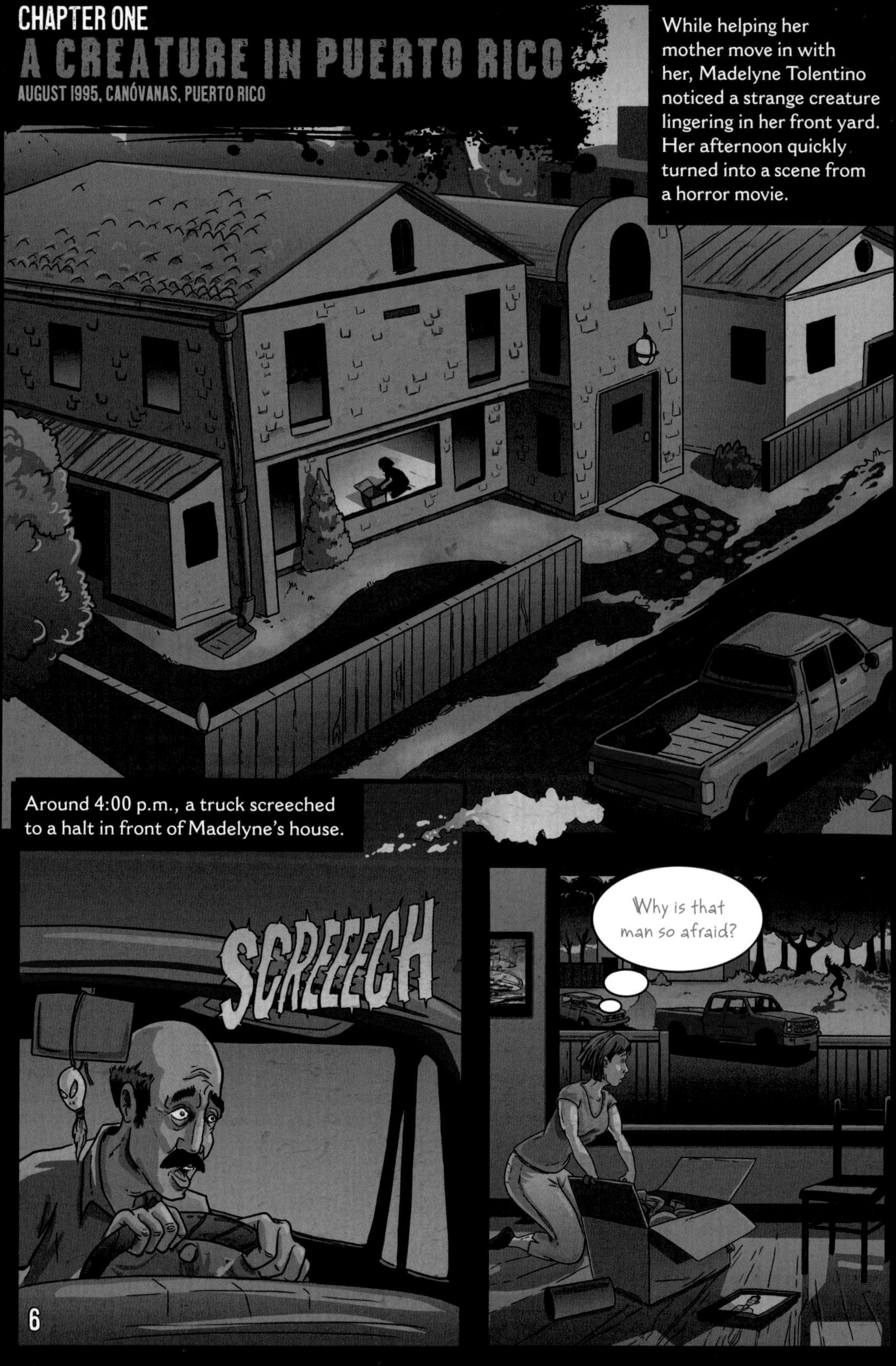
CHAPTER ONE
A CREATURE IN PUERTO RICO
AUGUST 1995, CANÓVANAS, PUERTO RICO
While helping her mother move in with her, Madelyne Tolentino noticed a strange creature lingering in her front yard. Her afternoon quickly turned into a scene from a horror movie.
Around 4:00 p.m., a truck screeched to a halt in front of Madelyne's house.
SCREECH
Why is that man so afraid?

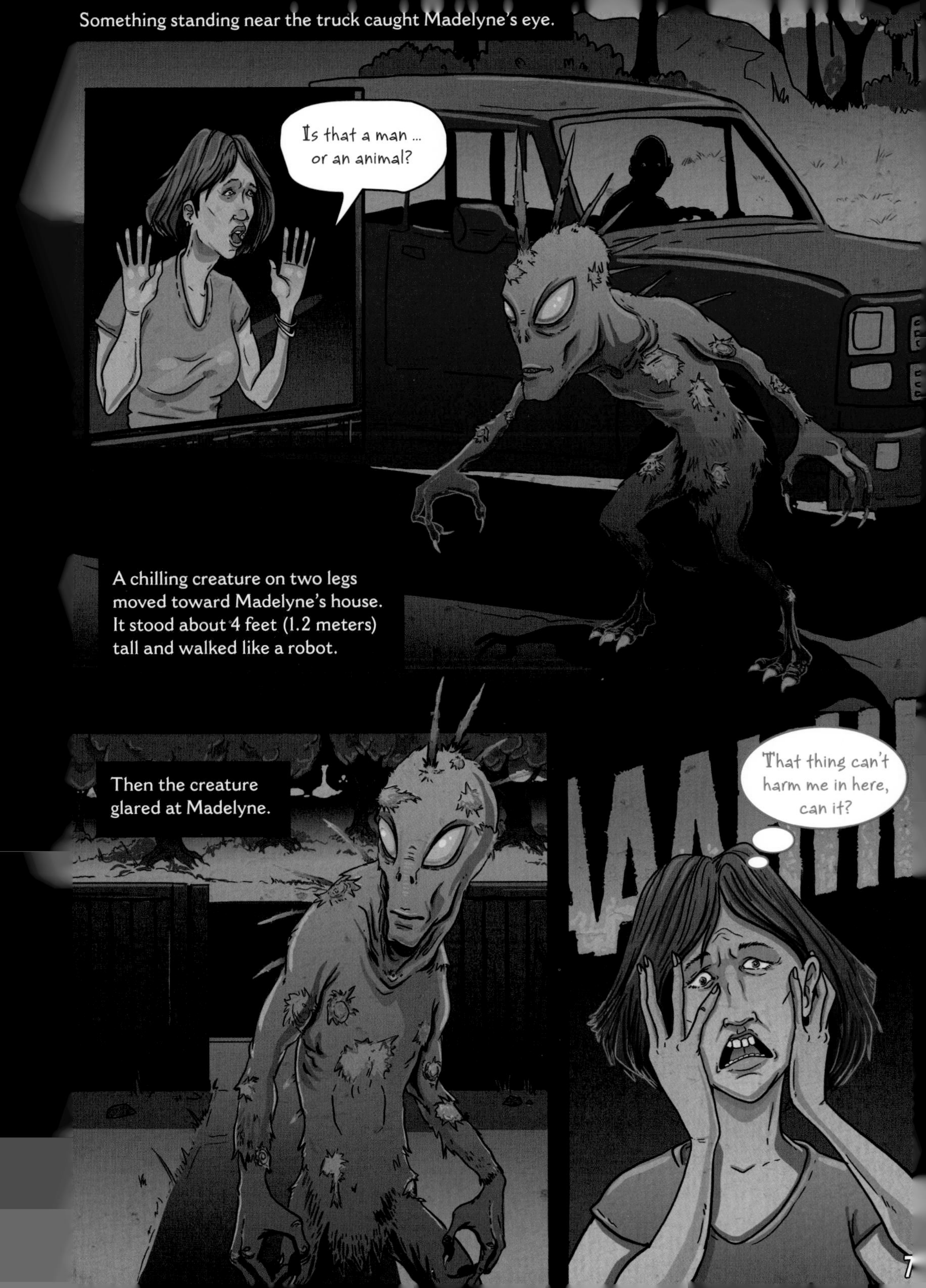
Something standing near the truck caught Madelyne's eye.
Is that a man ... or an animal?
A chilling creature on two legs moved toward Madelyne's house. It stood about 4 feet (1.2 meters) tall and walked like a robot.
Then the creature glared at Madelyne.
That thing can't harm me in here, can it?

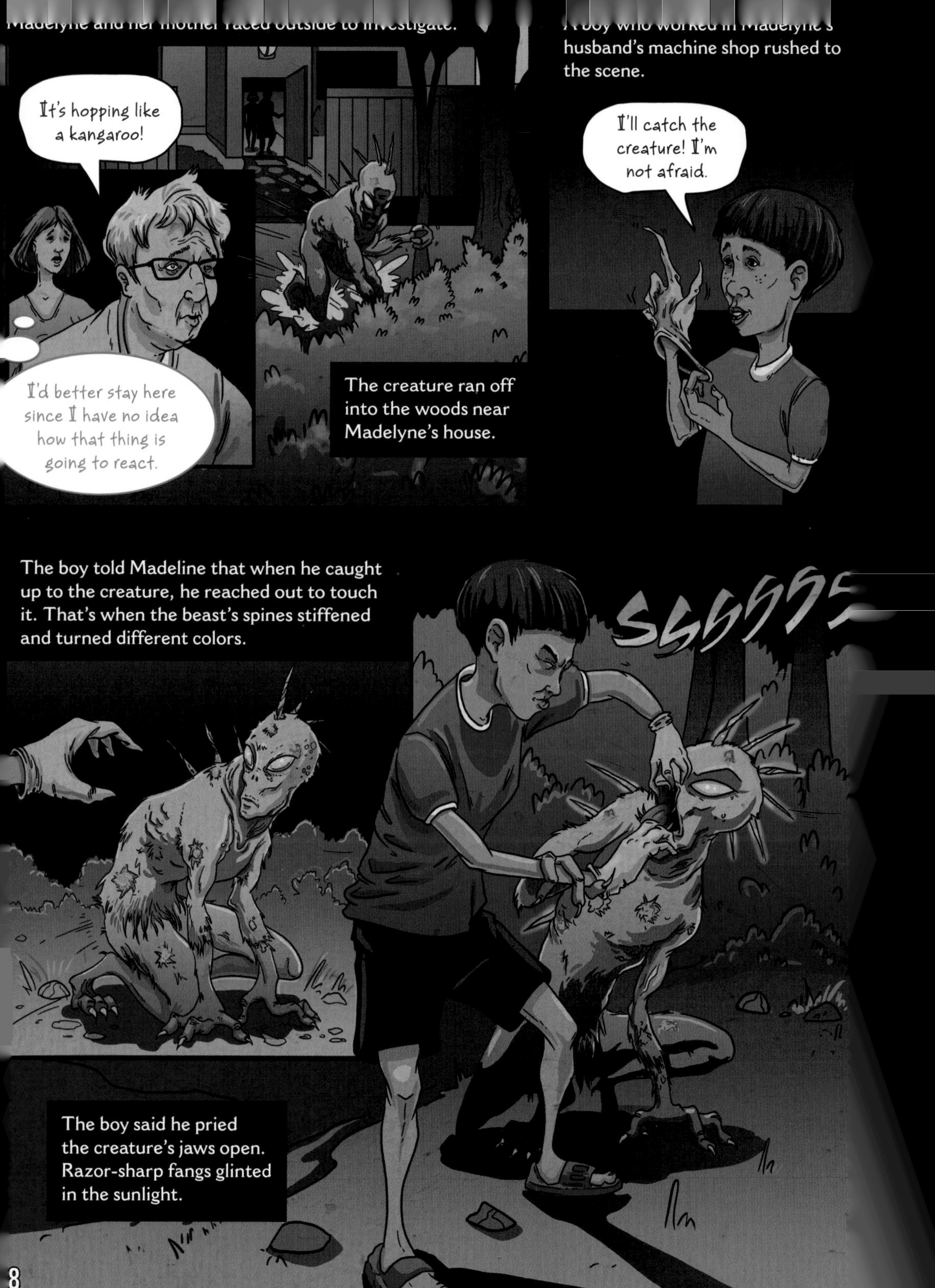
Madelyne and her mother raced outside to investigate.
It's hopping like a kangaroo!
I'd better stay here since I have no idea how that thing is going to react.
The creature ran off into the woods near Madelyne's house.
A boy who worked in Madelyne's husband's machine shop rushed to the scene.
I'll catch the creature! I'm not afraid.
The boy told Madeline that when he caught up to the creature, he reached out to touch it. That's when the beast's spines stiffened and turned different colors.
SSSSSS
The boy said he pried the creature's jaws open. Razor-sharp fangs glinted in the sunlight.

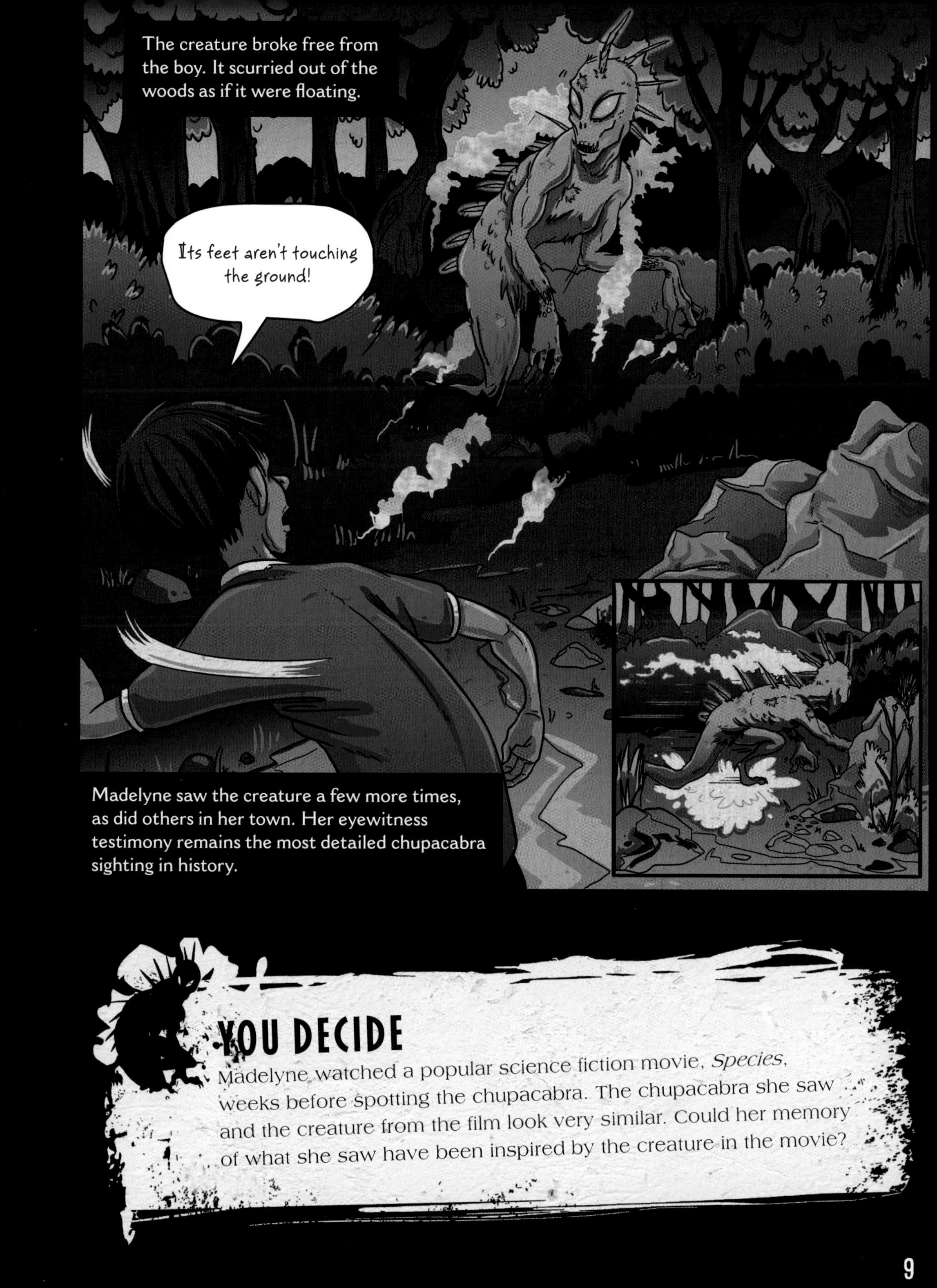
The creature broke free from the boy. It scurried out of the woods as if it were floating.
Its feet aren't touching the ground!
Madelyne saw the creature a few more times, as did others in her town. Her eyewitness testimony remains the most detailed chupacabra sighting in history.

YOU DECIDE

Madelyne watched a popular science fiction movie, *Species*, weeks before spotting the chupacabra. The chupacabra she saw and the creature from the film look very similar. Could her memory of what she saw have been inspired by the creature in the movie?

CHAPTER TWO

MYSTERY IN THE MOUNTAINS

SEPTEMBER 1998, CHINA

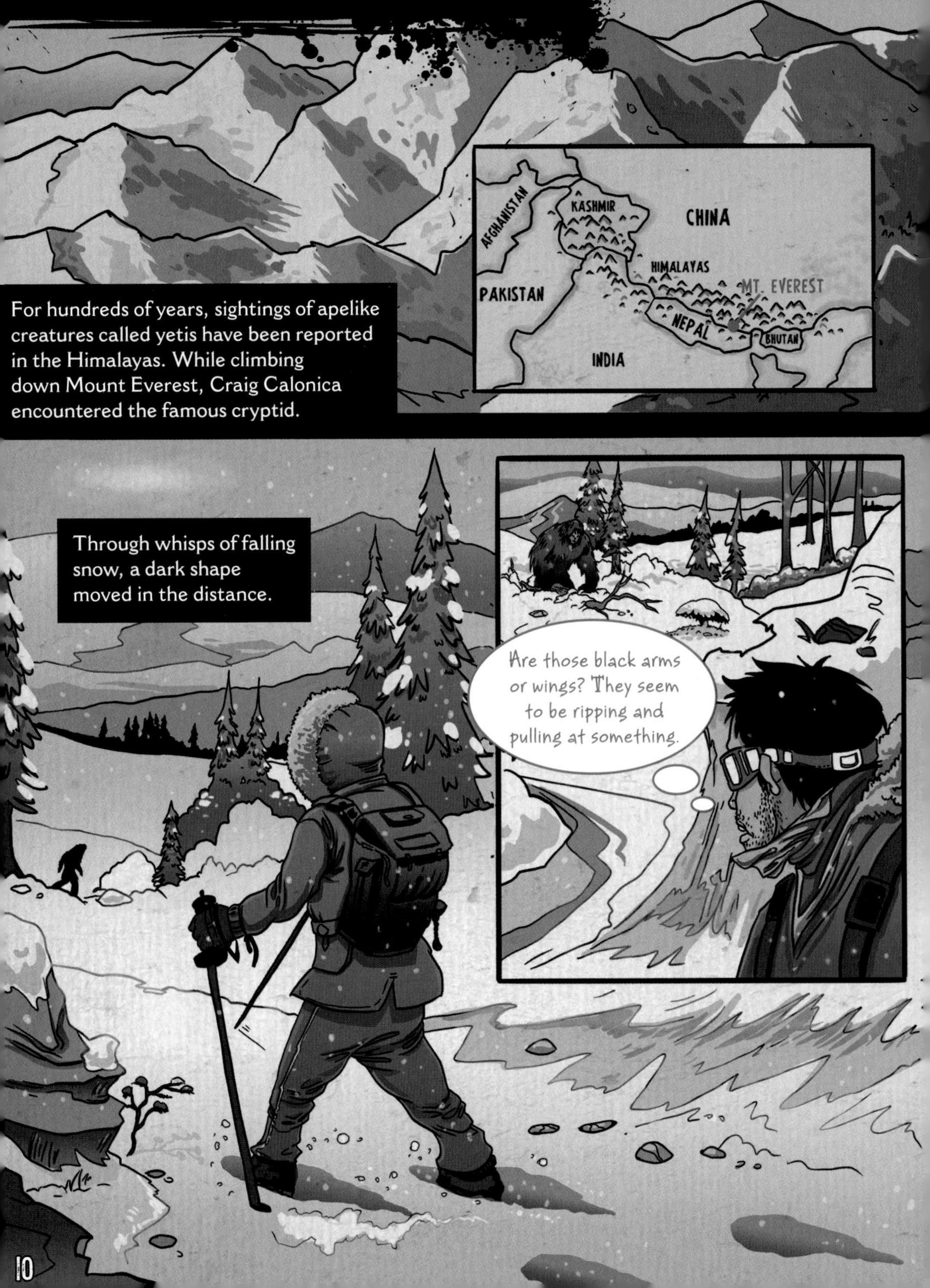
AFGHANISTAN
KASHMIR
CHINA
HIMALAYAS
PAKISTAN
MT. EVEREST
NEPAL
BHUTAN
INDIA
For hundreds of years, sightings of apelike creatures called yetis have been reported in the Himalayas. While climbing down Mount Everest, Craig Calonica encountered the famous cryptid.
Through whisps of falling snow, a dark shape moved in the distance.
Are those black arms or wings? They seem to be ripping and pulling at something.

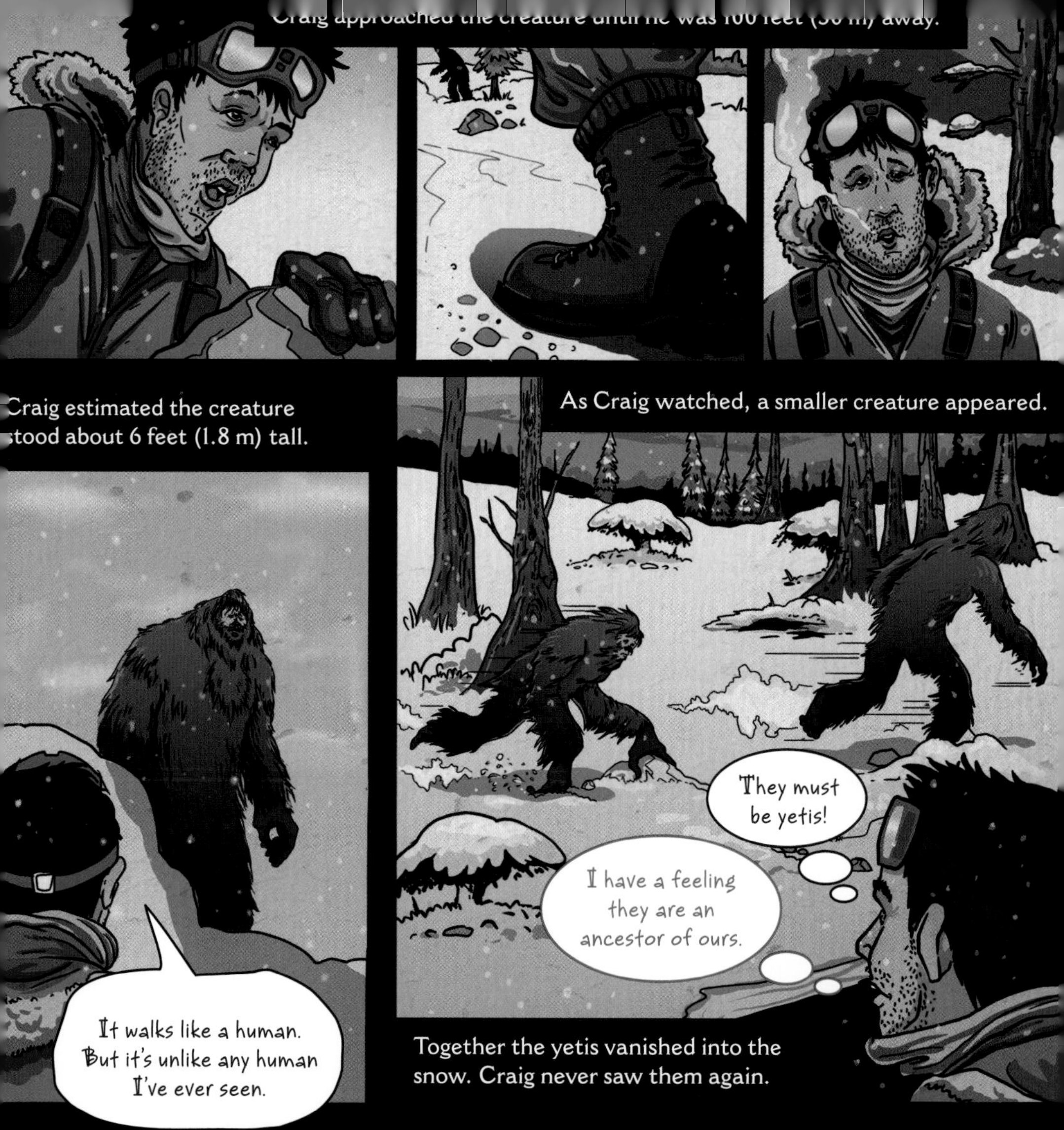
Craig approached the creature until he was 100 feet (30 m) away.
Craig estimated the creature stood about 6 feet (1.8 m) tall.
It walks like a human. But it's unlike any human I've ever seen.
As Craig watched, a smaller creature appeared.
They must be yetis!
I have a feeling they are an ancestor of ours.
Together the yetis vanished into the snow. Craig never saw them again.

YOU DECIDE

Mount Everest soars about 5.5 miles (8.9 kilometers) above sea level. It is the highest mountain in the world. Air at high altitudes contains less oxygen. When the brain does not receive enough oxygen, people can become confused or unable to walk straight. This condition is called altitude sickness. Yeti skeptics believe people like Craig Calonica suffered from altitude sickness during their sightings. They confuse bears or other animals for yetis. What do you think is true?

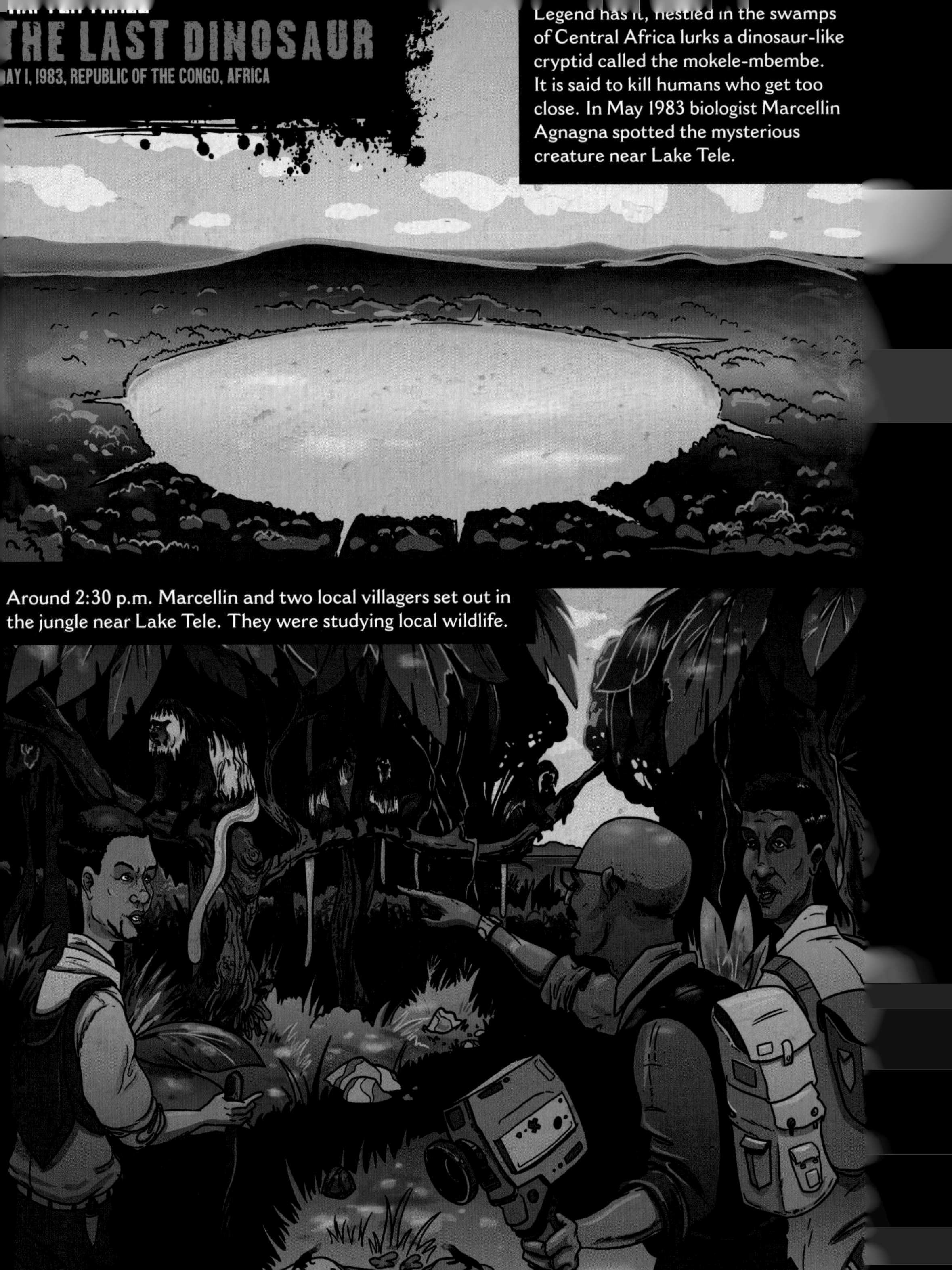
THE LAST DINOSAUR
AY 1, 1983, REPUBLIC OF THE CONGO, AFRICA
Legend has it, nestled in the swamps of Central Africa lurks a dinosaur-like cryptid called the mokele-mbembe. It is said to kill humans who get too close. In May 1983 biologist Marcellin Agnagna spotted the mysterious creature near Lake Tele.
Around 2:30 p.m. Marcellin and two local villagers set out in the jungle near Lake Tele. They were studying local wildlife.

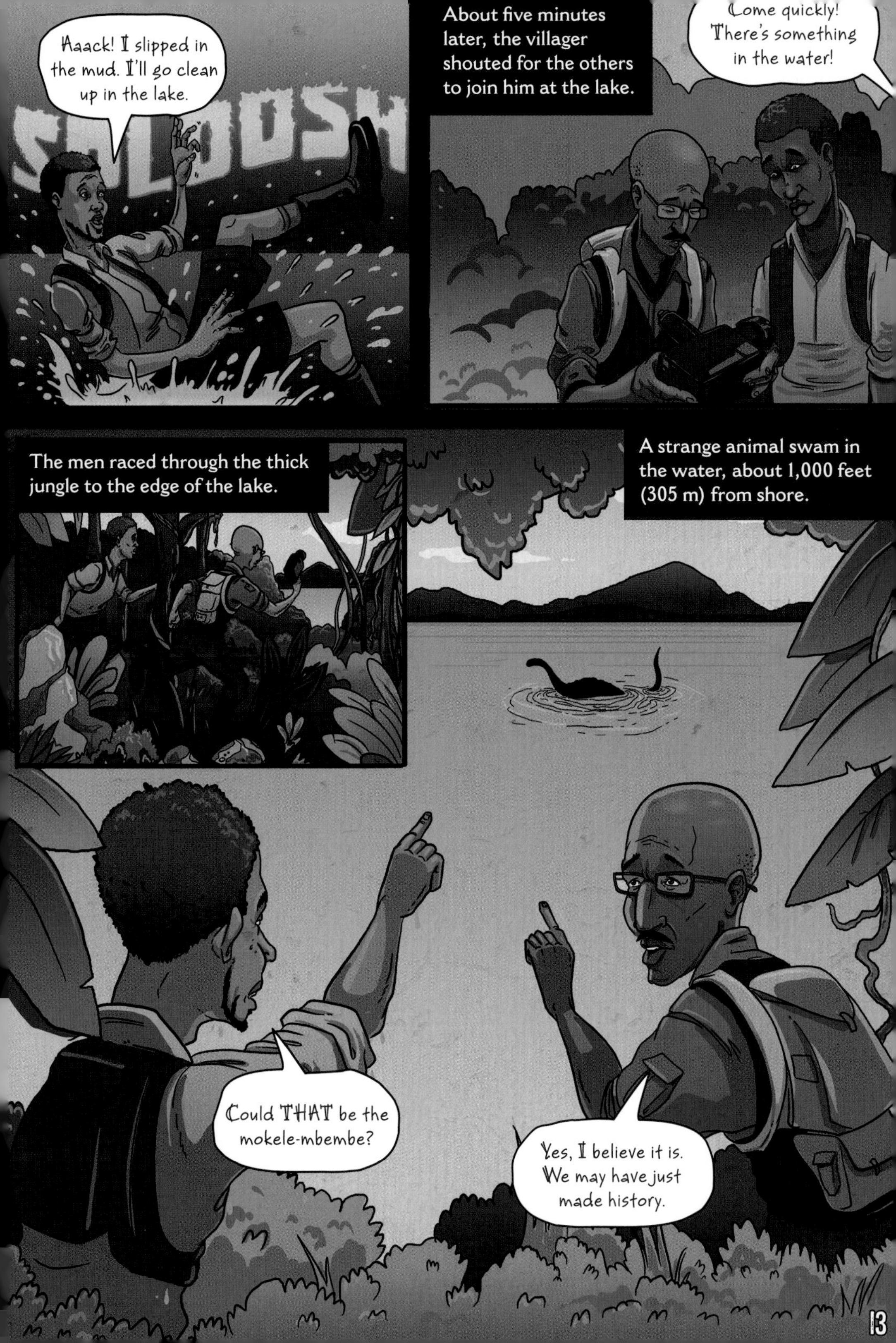
Aaack! I slipped in the mud. I'll go clean up in the lake.
SPLOOSH
About five minutes later, the villager shouted for the others to join him at the lake.
Come quickly! There's something in the water!
The men raced through the thick jungle to the edge of the lake.
A strange animal swam in the water, about 1,000 feet (305 m) from shore.
Could THAT be the mokele-mbembe?
Yes, I believe it is. We may have just made history.

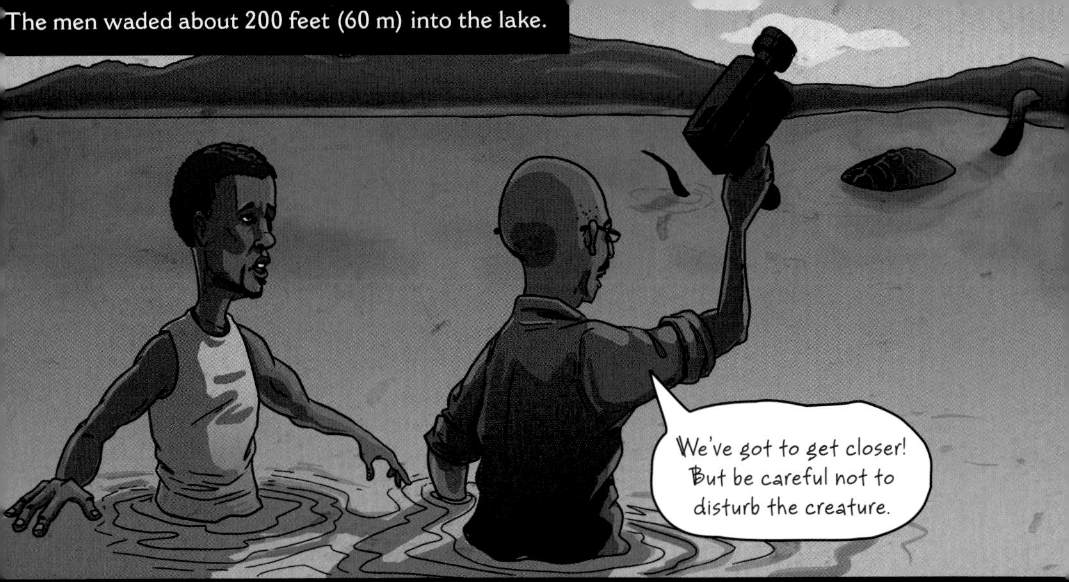
The men waded about 200 feet (60 m) into the lake.
We've got to get closer! But be careful not to disturb the creature.

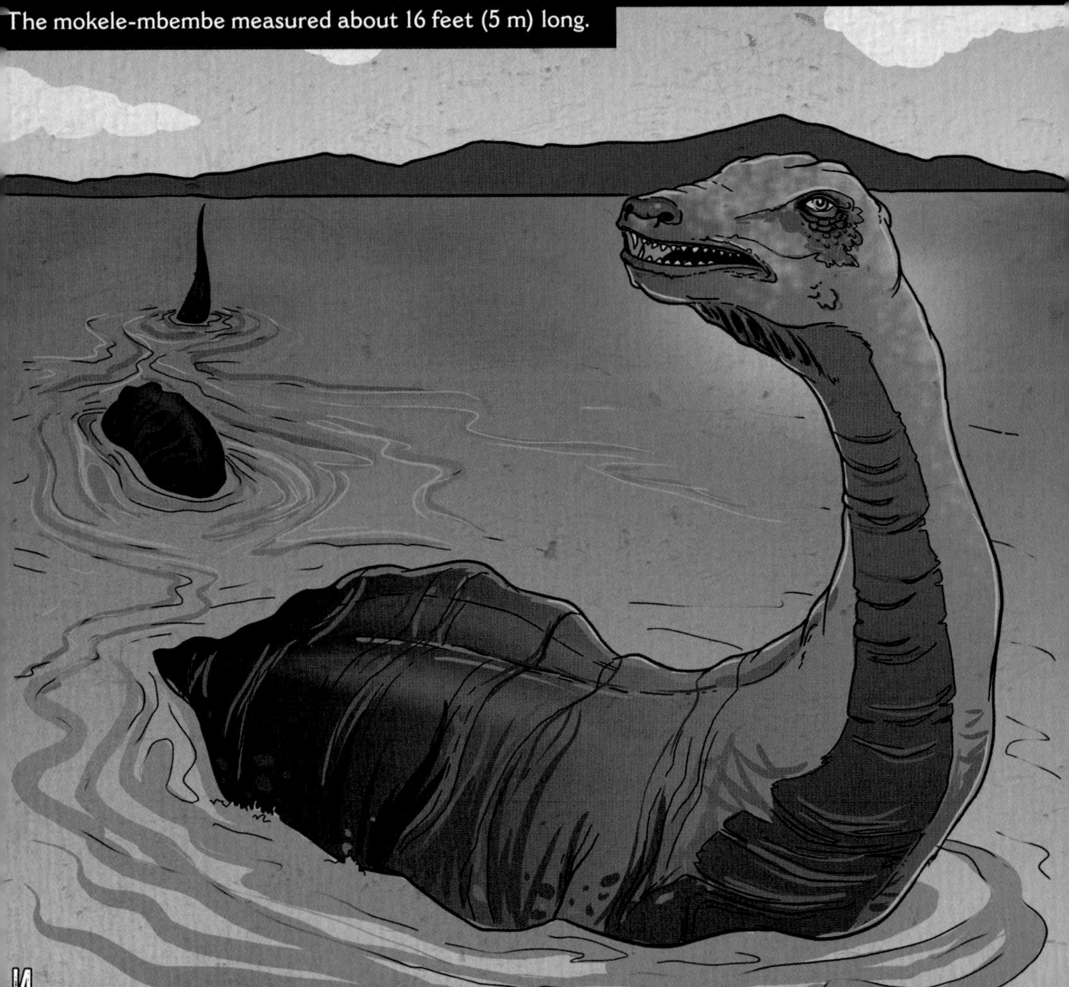
The mokele-mbembe measured about 16 feet (5 m) long.

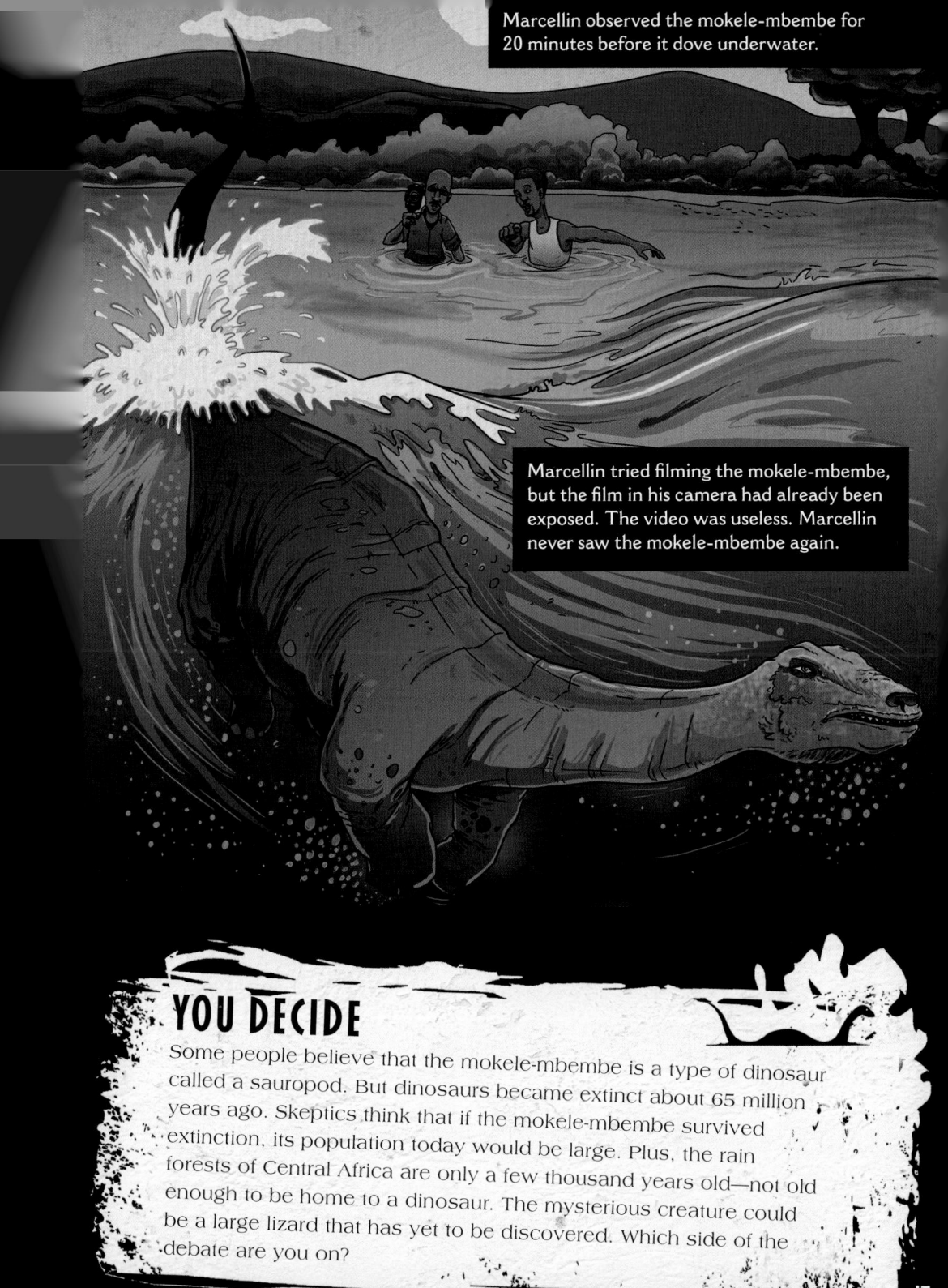

Marcellin observed the mokele-mbembe for 20 minutes before it dove underwater.

Marcellin tried filming the mokele-mbembe, but the film in his camera had already been exposed. The video was useless. Marcellin never saw the mokele-mbembe again.

YOU DECIDE

Some people believe that the mokele-mbembe is a type of dinosaur called a sauropod. But dinosaurs became extinct about 65 million years ago. Skeptics think that if the mokele-mbembe survived extinction, its population today would be large. Plus, the rain forests of Central Africa are only a few thousand years old—not old enough to be home to a dinosaur. The mysterious creature could be a large lizard that has yet to be discovered. Which side of the debate are you on?

CHAPTER FOUR

STRANGE NOISES

JANUARY 19, 1909, GLOUCESTER CITY, NEW JERSEY

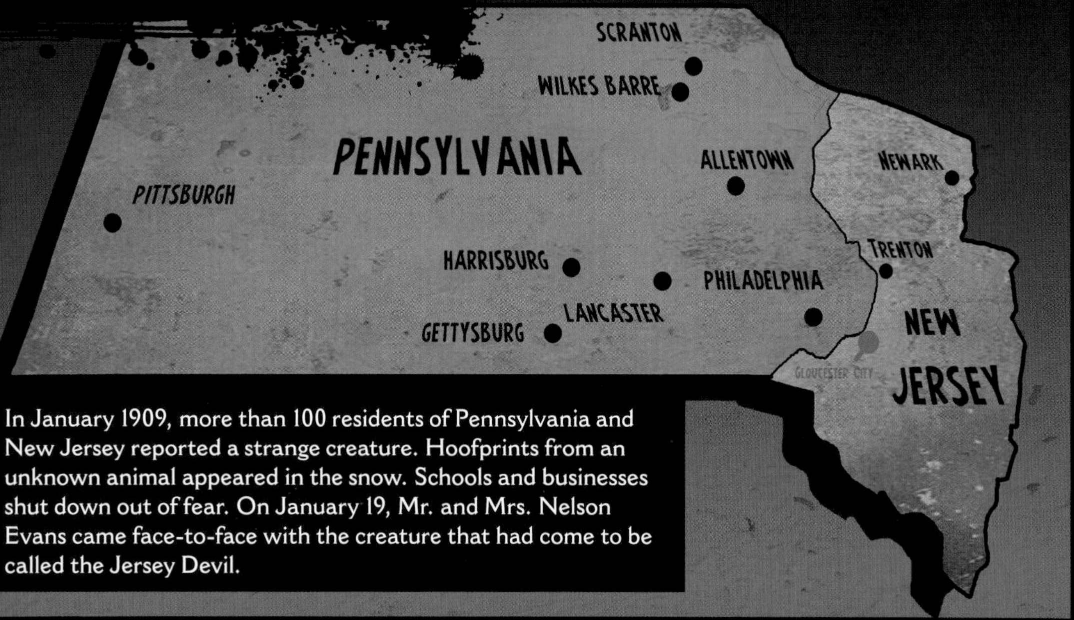
SCRANTON
WILKES BARRE
PENNSYLVANIA
ALLENTOWN
NEWARK
PITTSBURGH
TRENTON
HARRISBURG
PHILADELPHIA
LANCASTER
GETTYSBURG
NEW JERSEY
GLOUCESTER CITY

In January 1909, more than 100 residents of Pennsylvania and New Jersey reported a strange creature. Hoofprints from an unknown animal appeared in the snow. Schools and businesses shut down out of fear. On January 19, Mr. and Mrs. Nelson Evans came face-to-face with the creature that had come to be called the Jersey Devil.

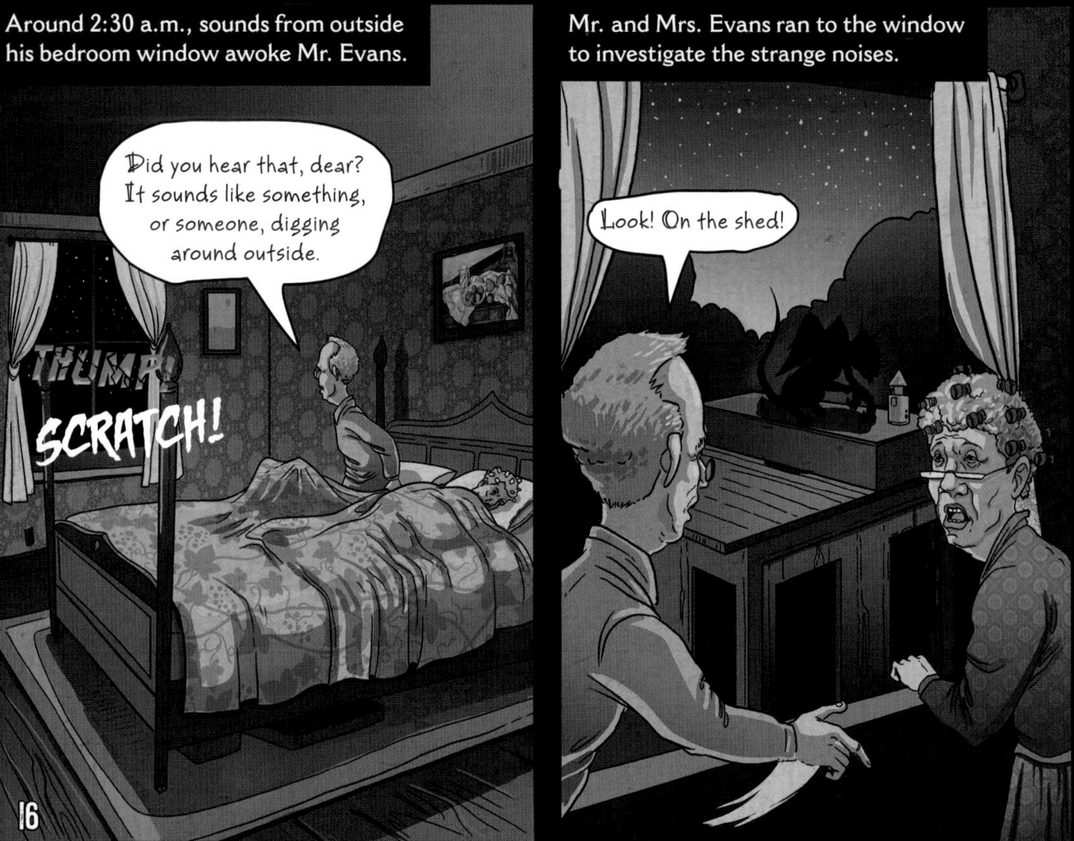
Around 2:30 a.m., sounds from outside his bedroom window awoke Mr. Evans.
Did you hear that, dear? It sounds like something, or someone, digging around outside.
THUMP!
SCRATCH!
Mr. and Mrs. Evans ran to the window to investigate the strange noises.
Look! On the shed!

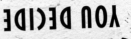

YOU DECIDE

During the 1909 sightings, Jacob Hope and Norman Jefferies painted a kangaroo green. They dressed it up with feathers and antlers and tricked people into paying to see a "Jersey Devil." In 1960, G.W. Green admitted to making some of the hoofprints in the snow. What do you think the Jersey Devil witnesses saw—a real-life monster or a hoax?

Mr. and Mrs. Evans watched the Jersey Devil for 10 minutes. The winged creature stood about 3 feet (1 m) tall. It walked on hooflike back feet.

Mr. Evans threw open the window and attempted to scare away the creature.

Shoo!

As the creature flapped its wings, Mrs. Evans heard a strange buzzing sound. Then the beast flew away.

Mr. and Mrs. Evans never saw the Jersey Devil again, but others did. By February the sightings ended.

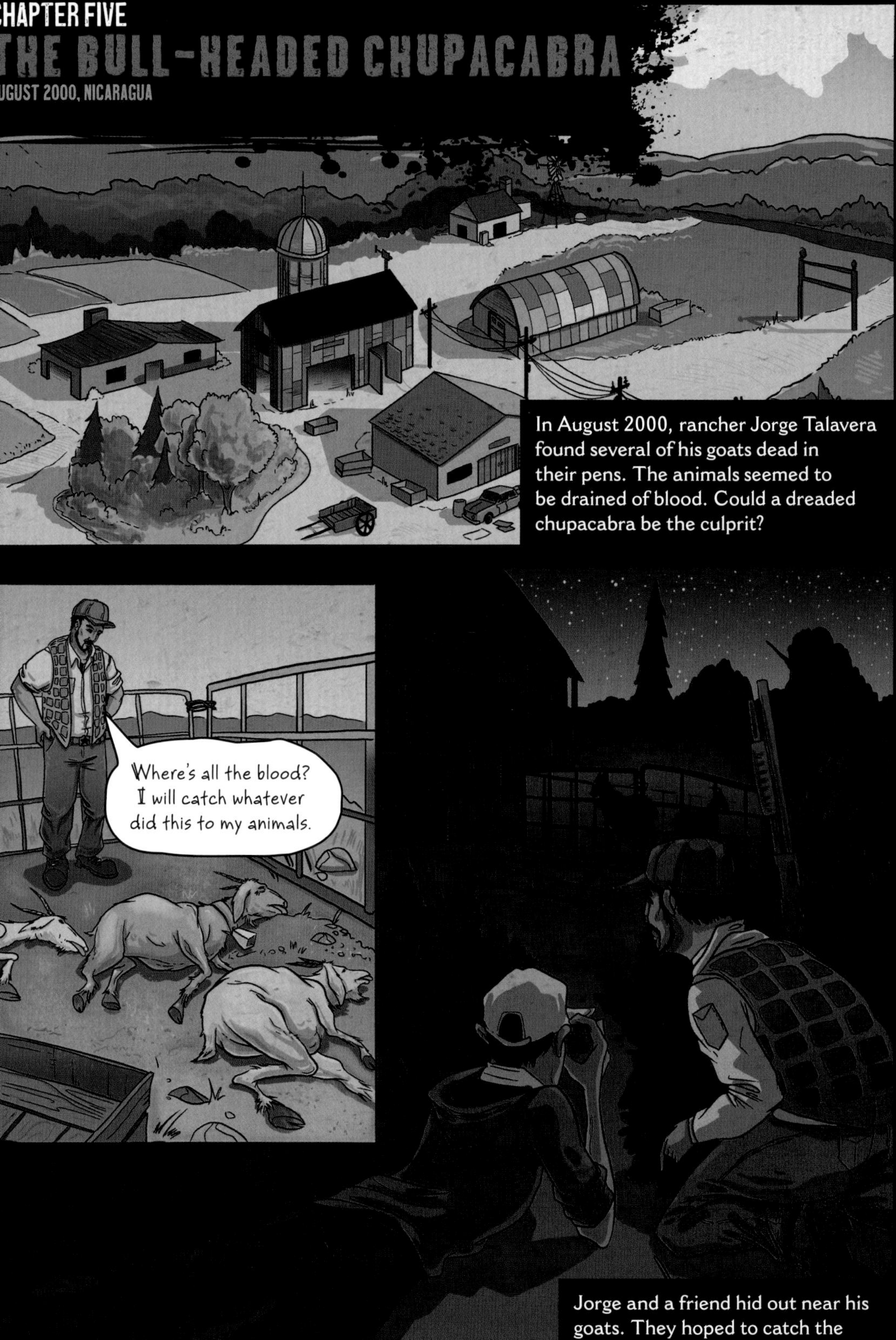
CHAPTER FIVE
THE BULL-HEADED CHUPACABRA
AUGUST 2000, NICARAGUA
In August 2000, rancher Jorge Talavera found several of his goats dead in their pens. The animals seemed to be drained of blood. Could a dreaded chupacabra be the culprit?
Where's all the blood? I will catch whatever did this to my animals.
Jorge and a friend hid out near his goats. They hoped to catch the

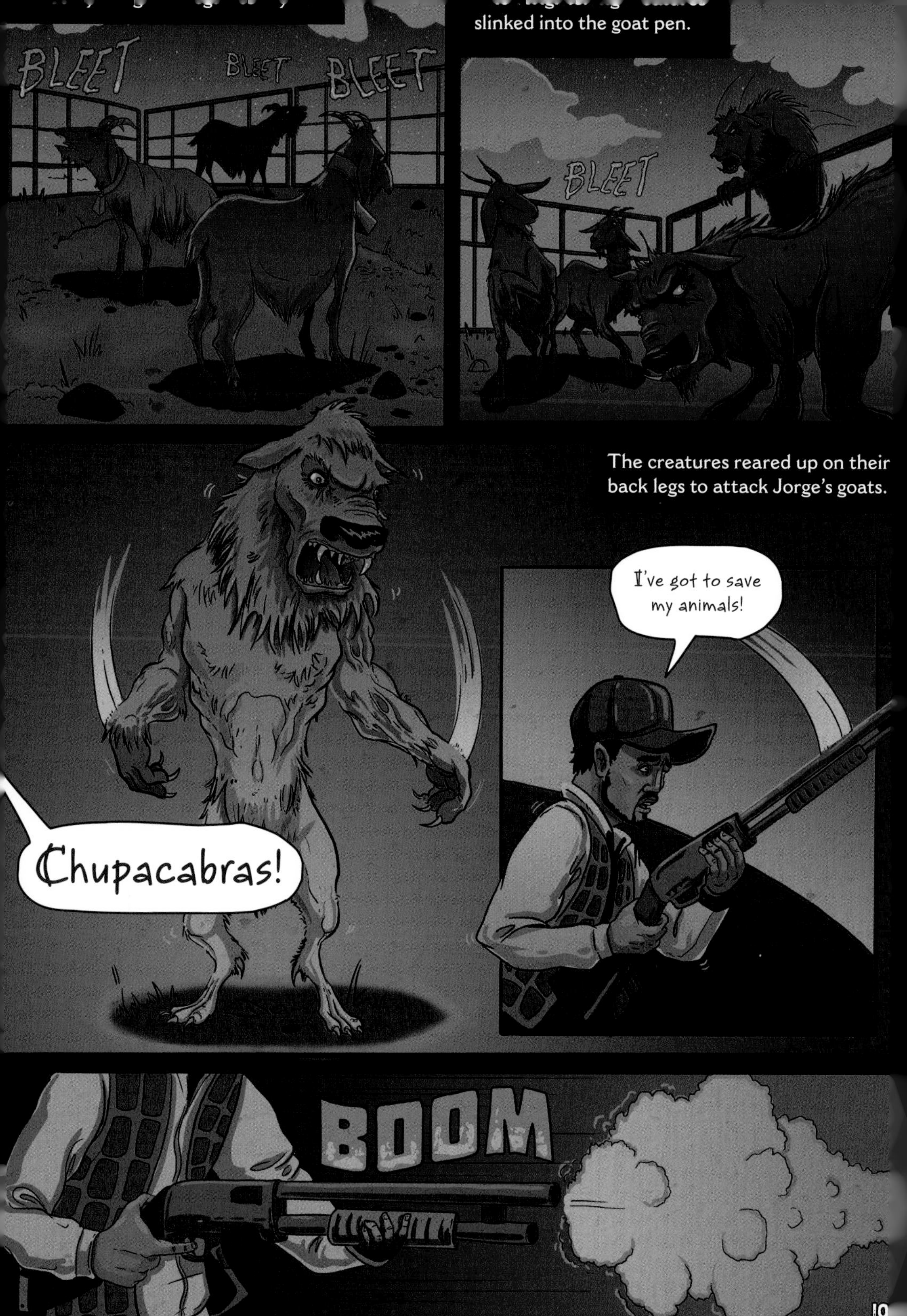
BLEET
BLEET
BLEET
slinked into the goat pen.
BLEET
The creatures reared up on their back legs to attack Jorge's goats.
Chupacabras!
I've got to save my animals!
BOOM

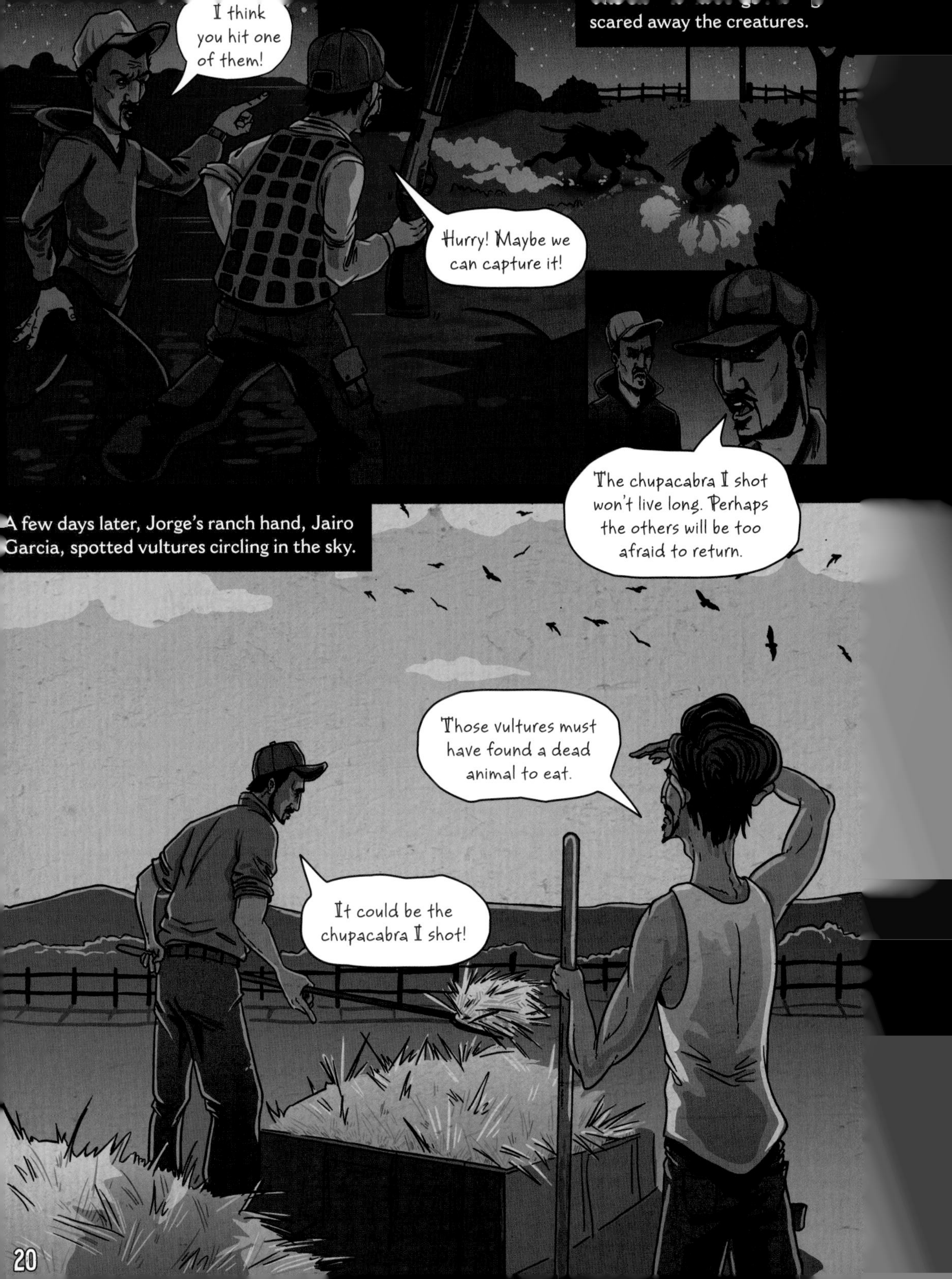
scared away the creatures.
I think you hit one of them!
Hurry! Maybe we can capture it!
The chupacabra I shot won't live long. Perhaps the others will be too afraid to return.
A few days later, Jorge's ranch hand, Jairo Garcia, spotted vultures circling in the sky.
Those vultures must have found a dead animal to eat.
It could be the chupacabra I shot!

Jairo and Jorge tracked the vultures to a small cave near the ranch. Rotting flesh and fur lay just inside the cave. The remains resembled the chupacabra that attacked Jorge's goats.

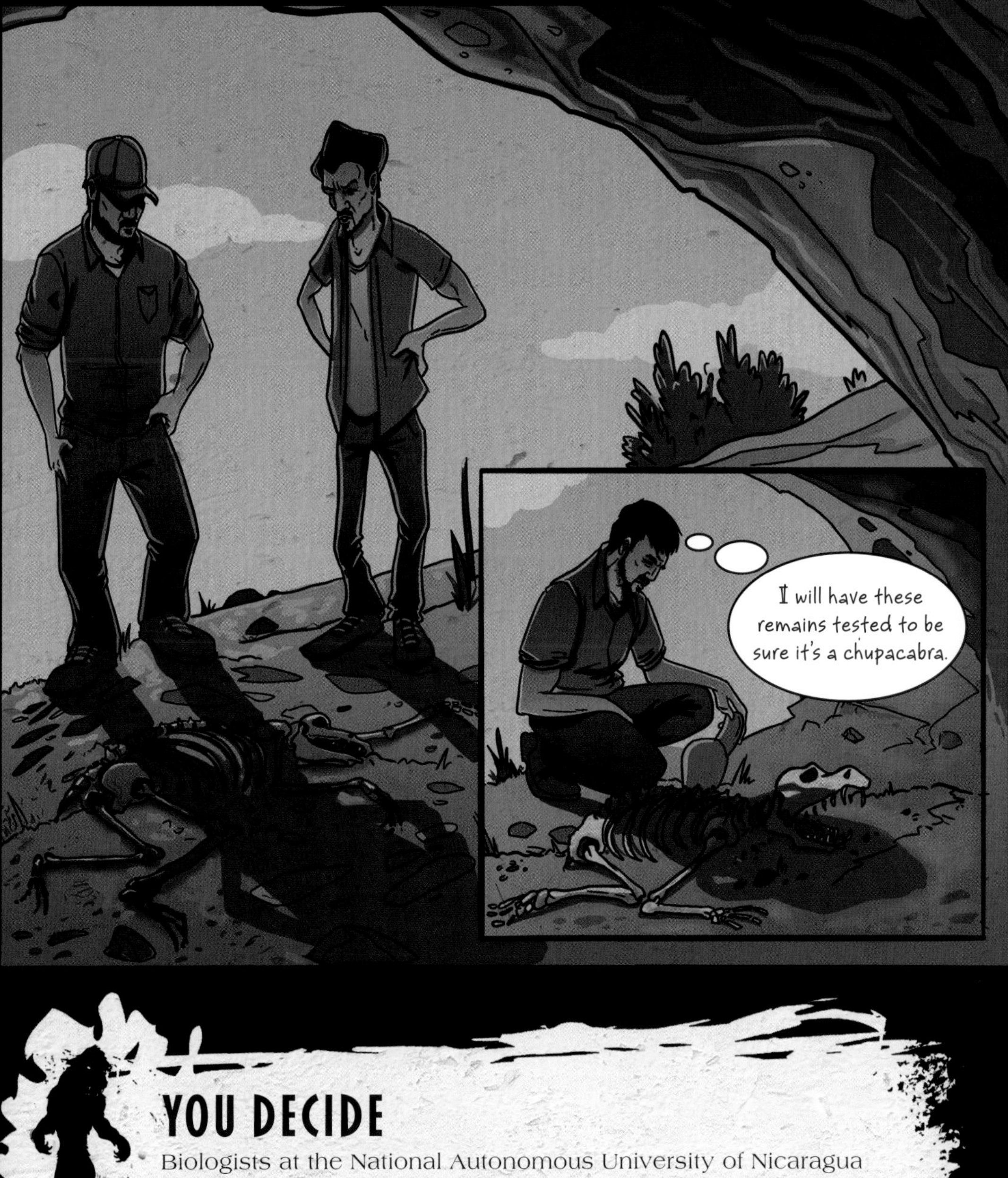
I will have these remains tested to be sure it's a chupacabra.

YOU DECIDE

Biologists at the National Autonomous University of Nicaragua examined the remains Jorge found. They found that the remains belonged to a common dog. The creature also had no fangs with which to suck blood. Jorge accused the biologists of covering up the truth. Who do you think has the right idea about this "chupacabra"—Jorge or the scientists?

CHAPTER SIX

MONSTER IN THE LOCH

JULY 22, 1933, SCOTLAND

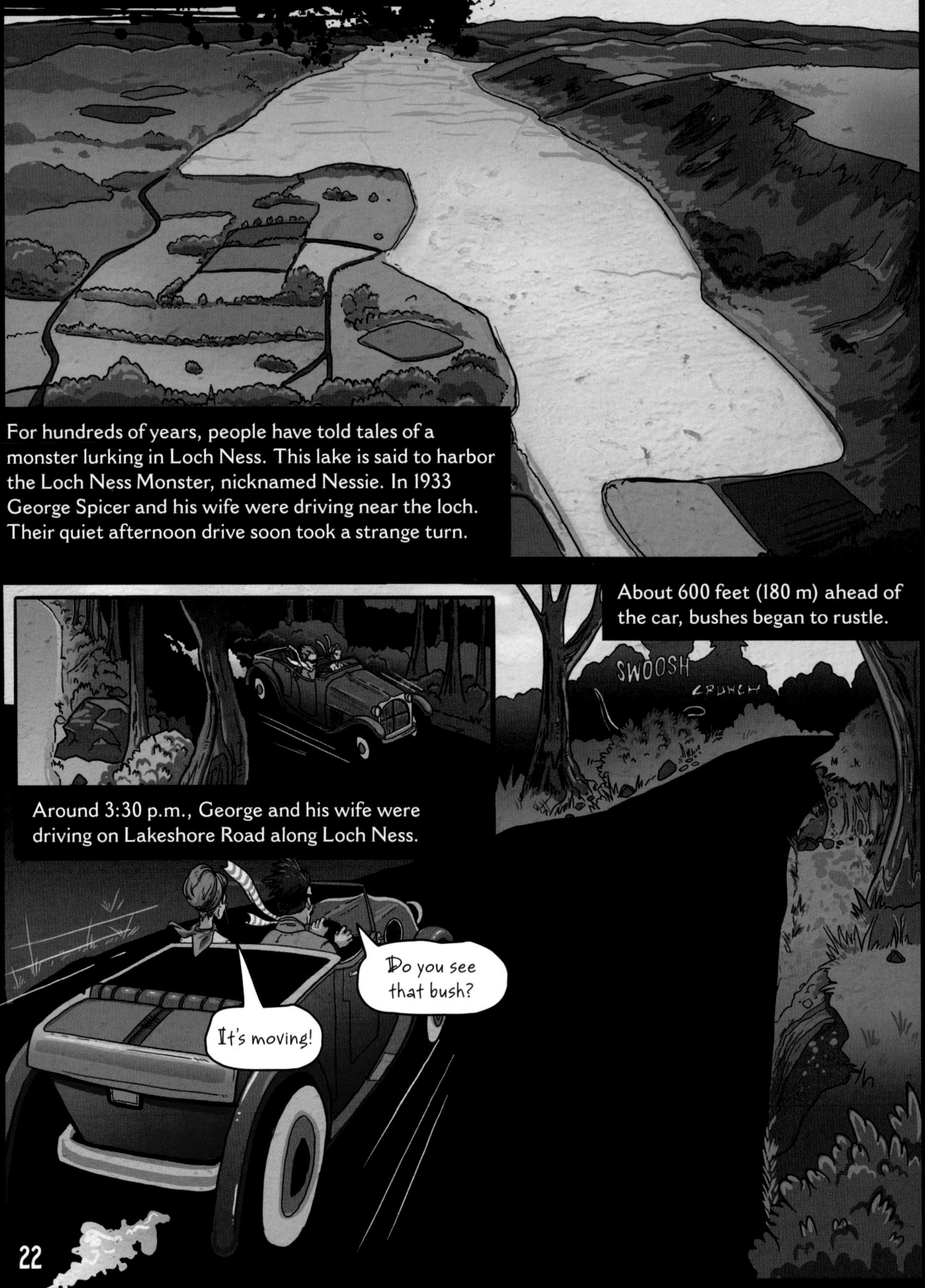
For hundreds of years, people have told tales of a monster lurking in Loch Ness. This lake is said to harbor the Loch Ness Monster, nicknamed Nessie. In 1933 George Spicer and his wife were driving near the loch. Their quiet afternoon drive soon took a strange turn.
Around 3:30 p.m., George and his wife were driving on Lakeshore Road along Loch Ness.
Do you see that bush?
It's moving!
About 600 feet (180 m) ahead of the car, bushes began to rustle.
SWOOSH
CRUNCH

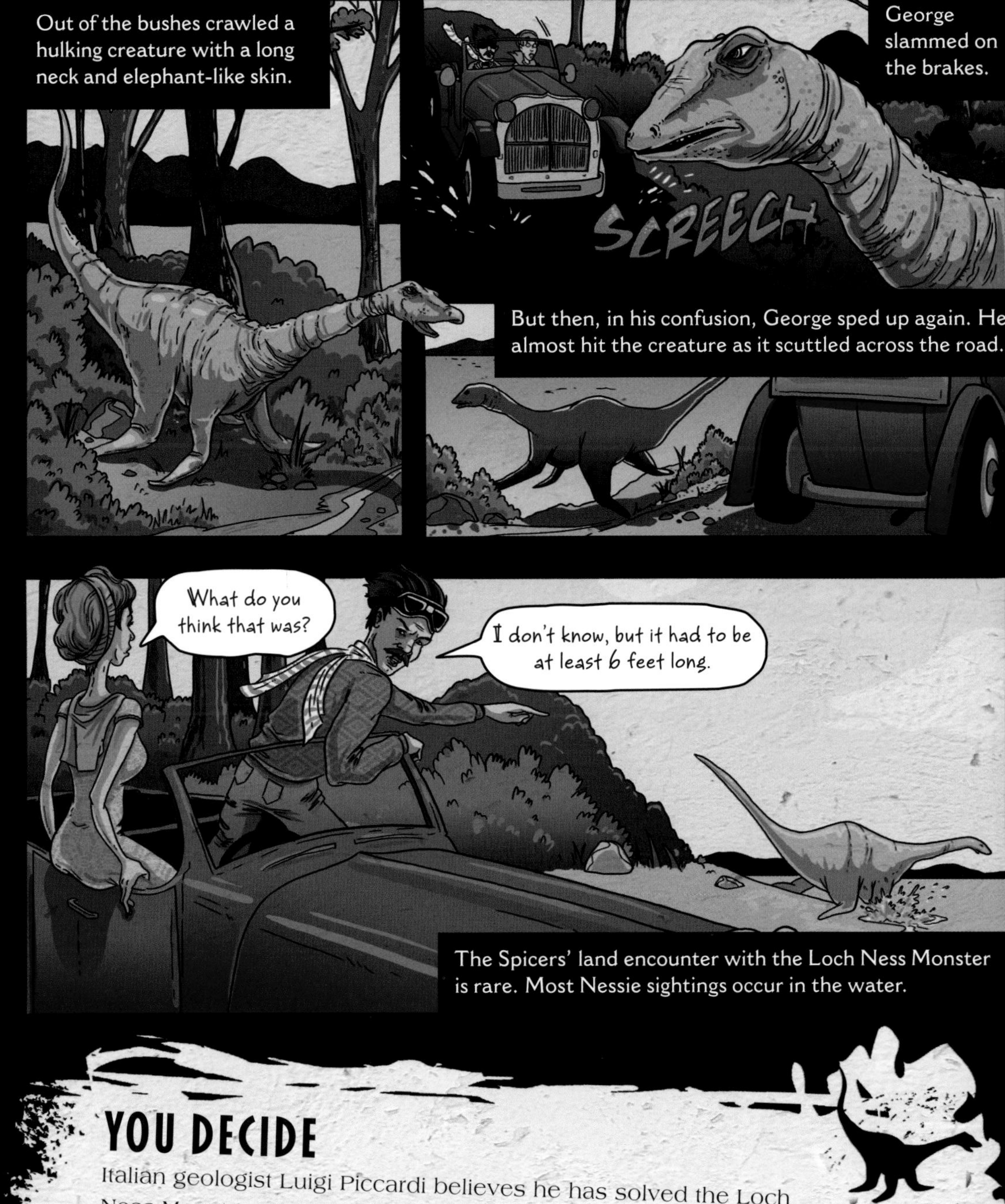
Out of the bushes crawled a hulking creature with a long neck and elephant-like skin.
George slammed on the brakes.
SCREECH
But then, in his confusion, George sped up again. He almost hit the creature as it scuttled across the road.
What do you think that was?
I don't know, but it had to be at least 6 feet long.
The Spicers' land encounter with the Loch Ness Monster is rare. Most Nessie sightings occur in the water.

YOU DECIDE

Italian geologist Luigi Piccardi believes he has solved the Loch Ness Monster mystery. The loch sits on the Great Glen fault line, a large crack in the Earth that can cause earthquakes. Piccardi says small shocks created by the fault line cause bubbles in the water. People mistake these bubbles for the Loch Ness Monster. Skeptics have also explained the Spicers' land encounter. They believe they saw a large otter crossing the road. Could the Loch Ness sightings be so easily explained?

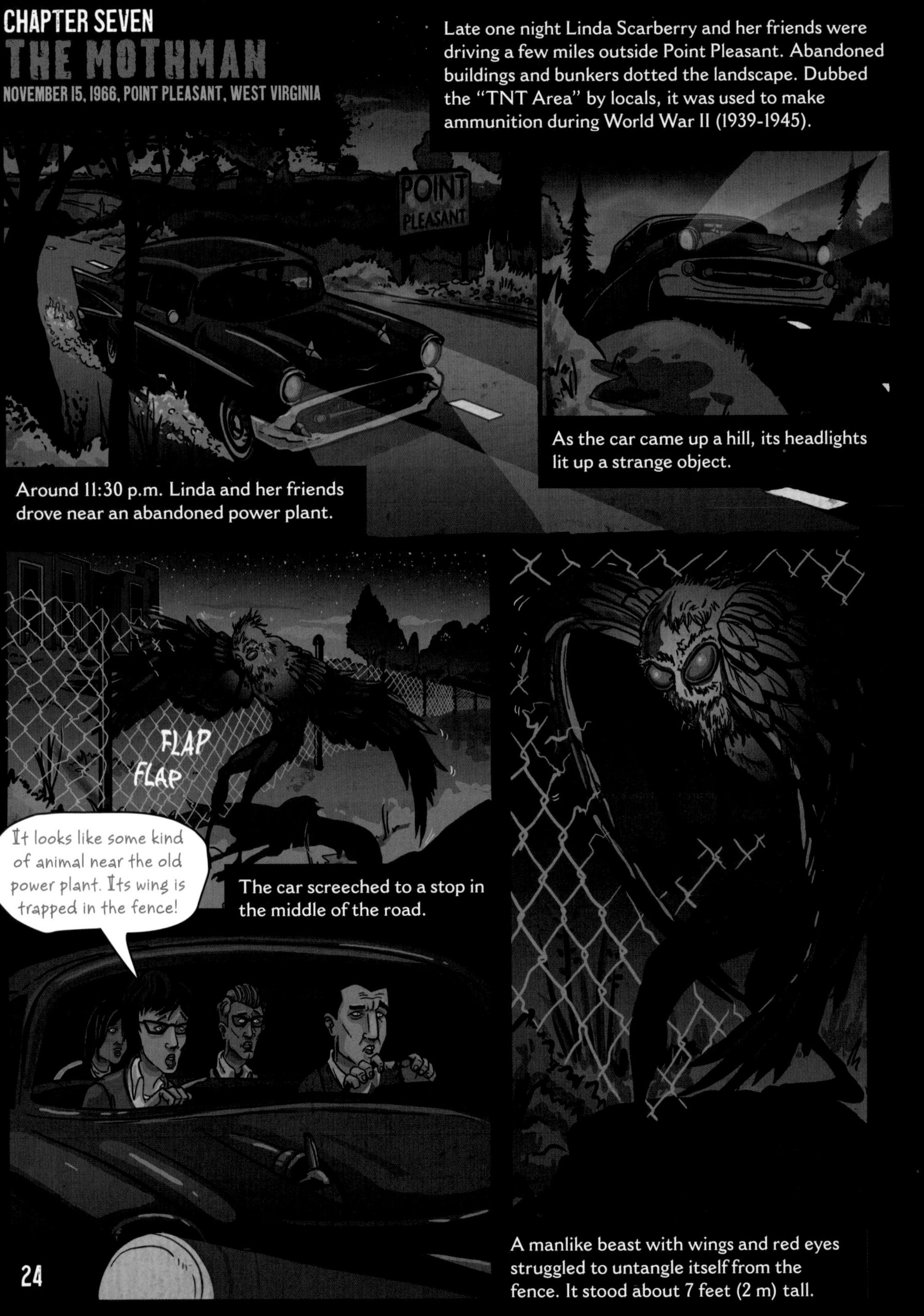
CHAPTER SEVEN
THE MOTHMAN
NOVEMBER 15, 1966, POINT PLEASANT, WEST VIRGINIA
Late one night Linda Scarberry and her friends were driving a few miles outside Point Pleasant. Abandoned buildings and bunkers dotted the landscape. Dubbed the "TNT Area" by locals, it was used to make ammunition during World War II (1939-1945).
POINT PLEASANT
As the car came up a hill, its headlights lit up a strange object.
Around 11:30 p.m. Linda and her friends drove near an abandoned power plant.
FLAP
FLAP
It looks like some kind of animal near the old power plant. Its wing is trapped in the fence!
The car screeched to a stop in the middle of the road.
A manlike beast with wings and red eyes struggled to untangle itself from the fence. It stood about 7 feet (2 m) tall.

Once the creature freed itself, it hobbled behind the power plant.

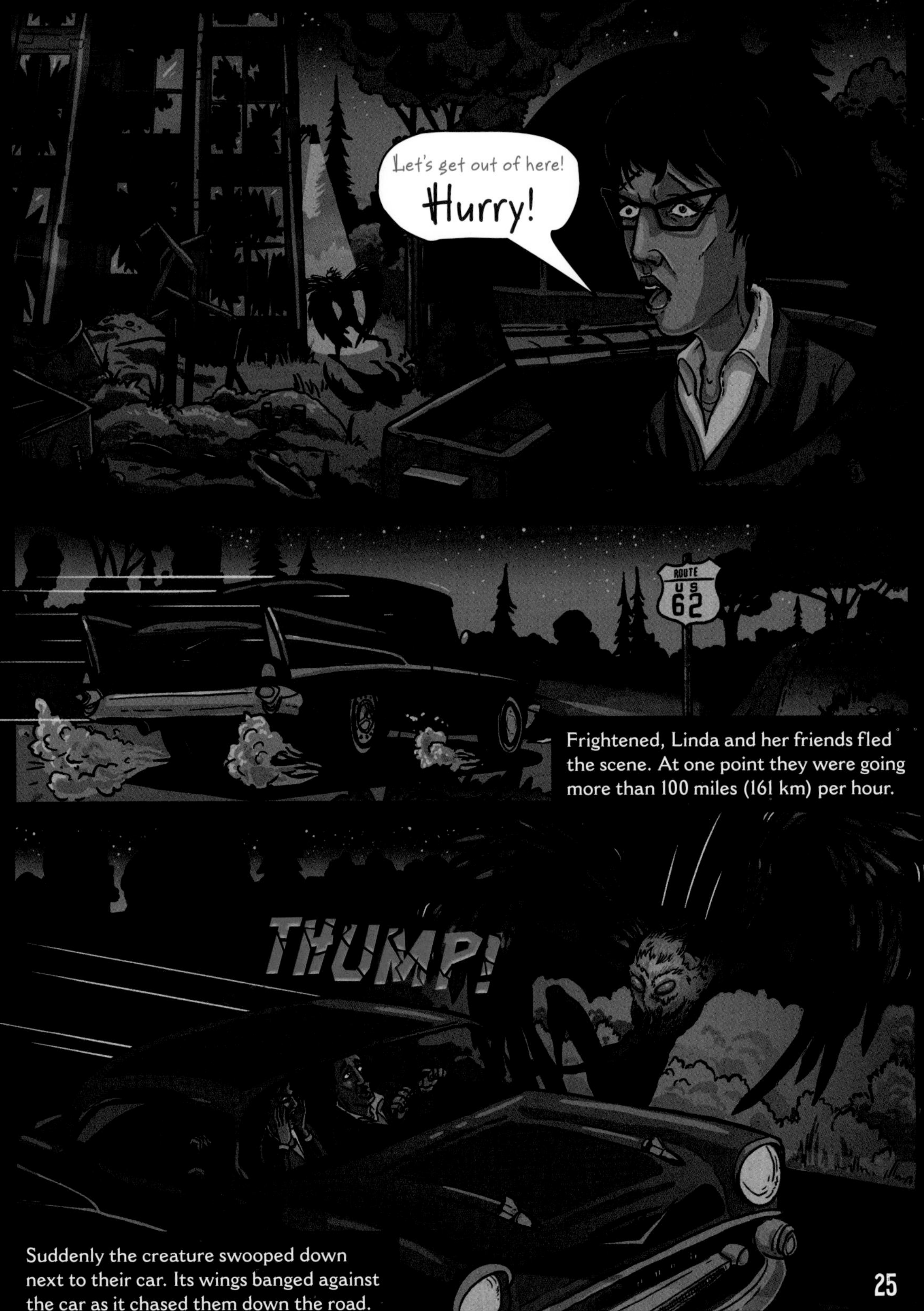
Let's get out of here!
Hurry!
ROUTE US 62
THUMP!

Frightened, Linda and her friends fled the scene. At one point they were going more than 100 miles (161 km) per hour.

Suddenly the creature swooped down next to their car. Its wings banged against the car as it chased them down the road.

Once the car reached the lighted gate of a farm, the creature flew away. It seemed to be afraid of the light.

Linda and her friends drove to a drive-in movie theater in Point Pleasant. They decided to ask the police for help.

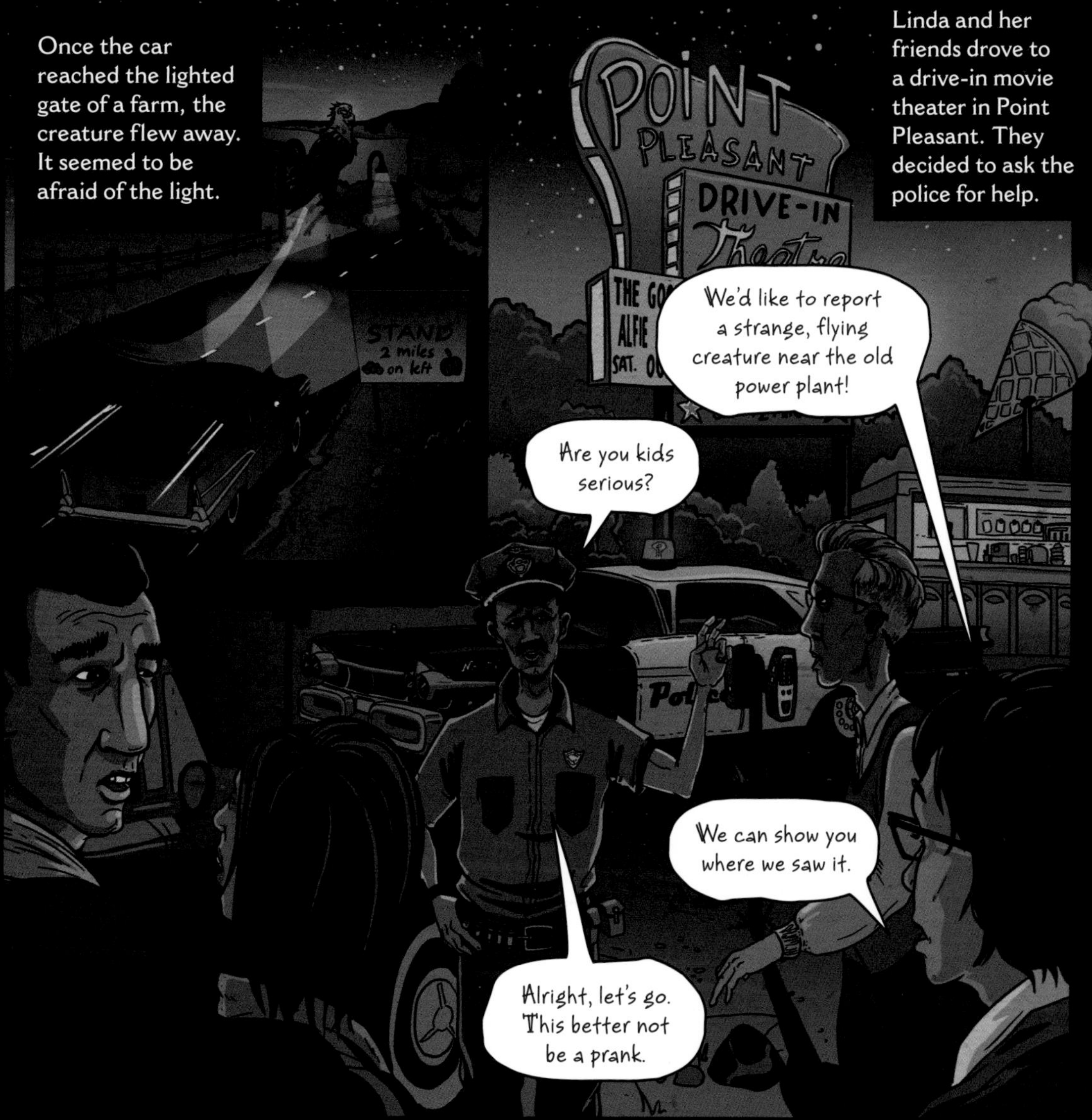
STAND
2 miles on left
POINT PLEASANT
DRIVE-IN
Theatre
We'd like to report a strange, flying creature near the old power plant!
Are you kids serious?
We can show you where we saw it.
Alright, let's go. This better not be a prank.

The police officers followed about half a mile behind Linda and her friends.

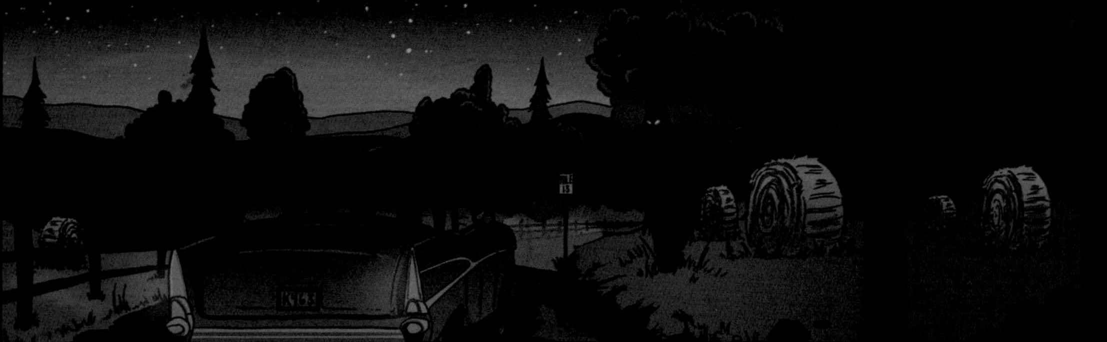

The creature seemed to be waiting for the friends in a pasture.

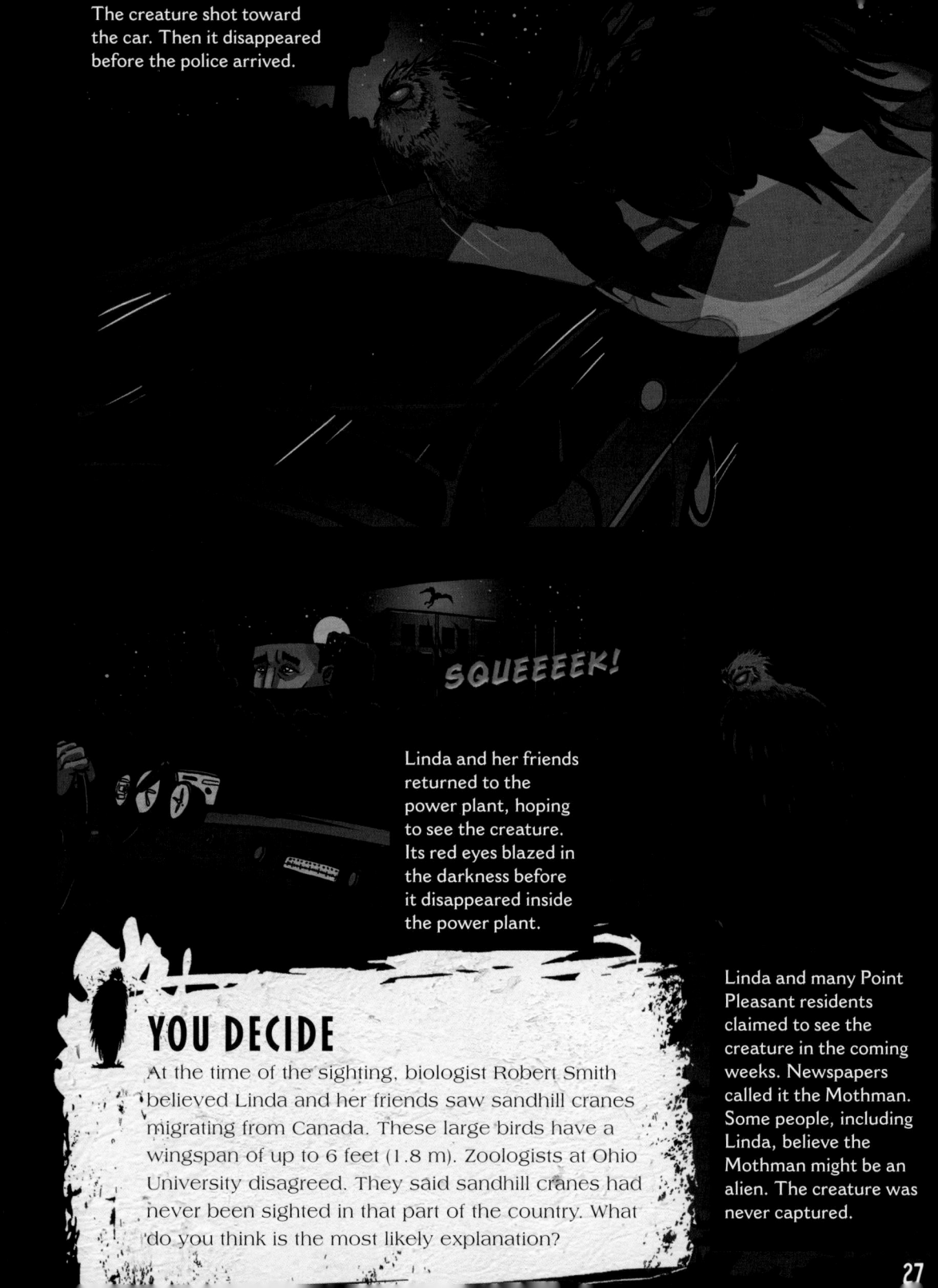

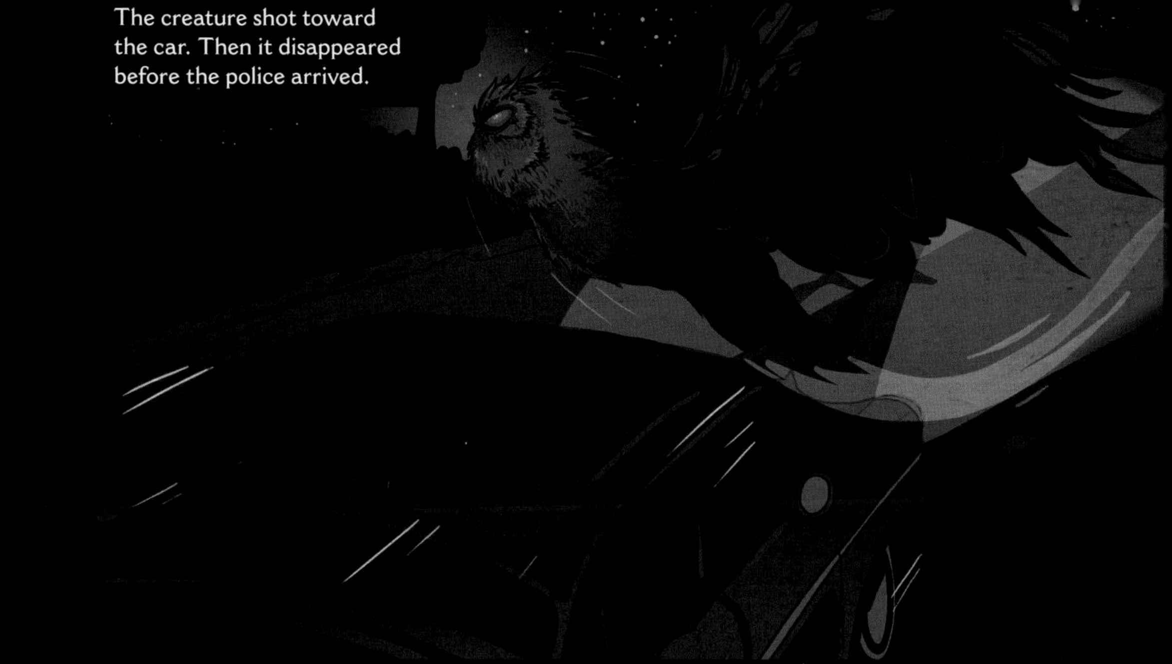
The creature shot toward the car. Then it disappeared before the police arrived.

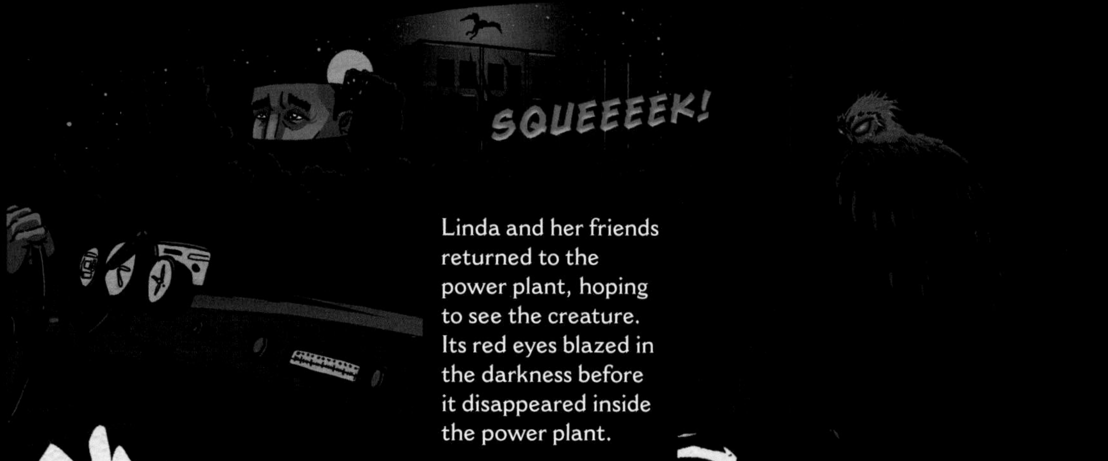
SQUEEEEEK!
Linda and her friends returned to the power plant, hoping to see the creature. Its red eyes blazed in the darkness before it disappeared inside the power plant.

YOU DECIDE

At the time of the sighting, biologist Robert Smith believed Linda and her friends saw sandhill cranes migrating from Canada. These large birds have a wingspan of up to 6 feet (1.8 m). Zoologists at Ohio University disagreed. They said sandhill cranes had never been sighted in that part of the country. What do you think is the most likely explanation?

Linda and many Point Pleasant residents claimed to see the creature in the coming weeks. Newspapers called it the Mothman. Some people, including Linda, believe the Mothman might be an alien. The creature was never captured.

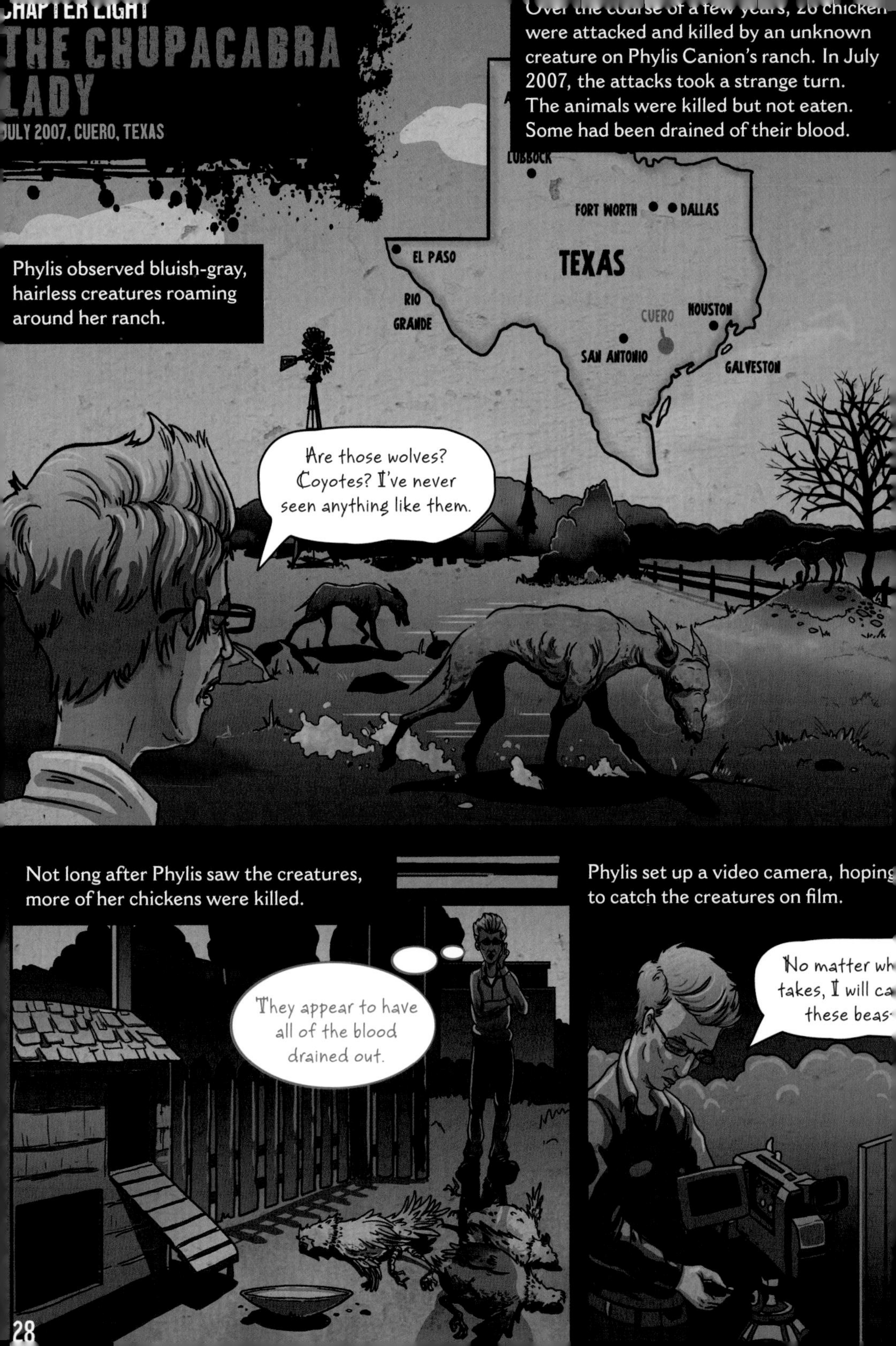
THE CHUPACABRA
LADY
JULY 2007, CUERO, TEXAS
were attacked and killed by an unknown creature on Phylis Canion's ranch. In July 2007, the attacks took a strange turn. The animals were killed but not eaten. Some had been drained of their blood.
LUBBOCK
FORT WORTH
DALLAS
EL PASO
TEXAS
RIO GRANDE
CUERO
HOUSTON
SAN ANTONIO
GALVESTON
Phylis observed bluish-gray, hairless creatures roaming around her ranch.
Are those wolves? Coyotes? I've never seen anything like them.
Not long after Phylis saw the creatures, more of her chickens were killed.
They appear to have all of the blood drained out.
Phylis set up a video camera, hoping to catch the creatures on film.

Before Phylis captured anything on video, a neighbor called her with important news.

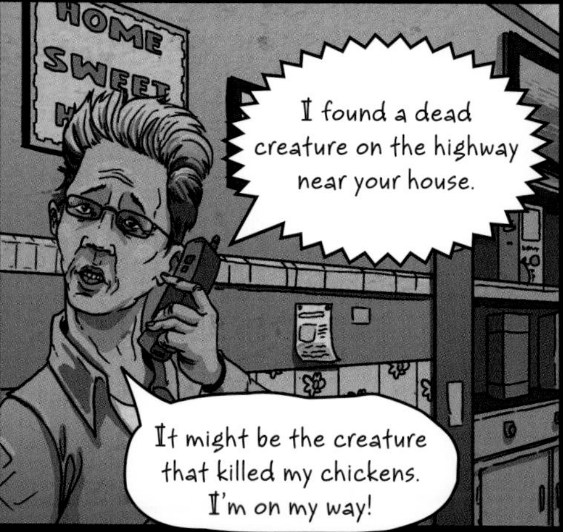
I found a dead creature on the highway near your house.
It might be the creature that killed my chickens. I'm on my way!

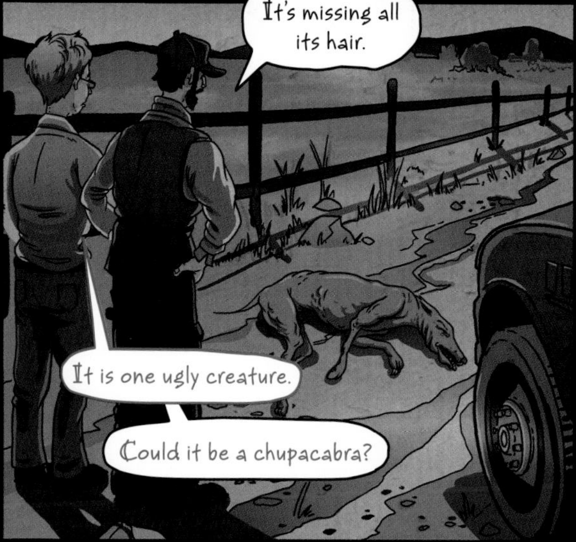
It's missing all its hair.
It is one ugly creature.
Could it be a chupacabra?

Phylis collected the chupacabra with her tractor and took it home.

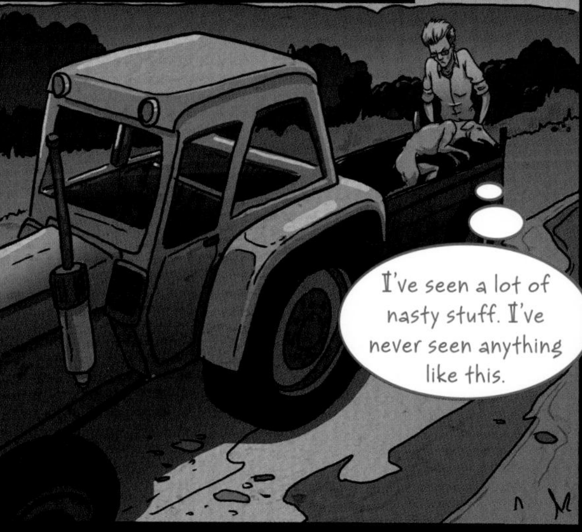
I've seen a lot of nasty stuff. I've never seen anything like this.

Phylis' photograph of the alleged chupacabra became famous around the world. It earned her the nickname "The Chupacabra Lady."

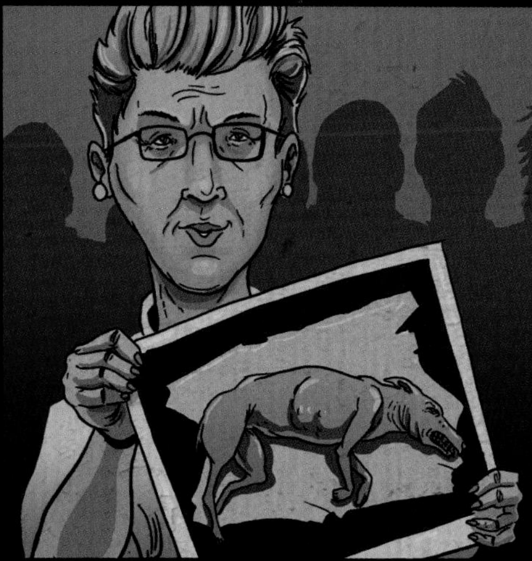

YOU DECIDE

Scientists at Texas State University tested skin and muscle fibers from the creature Phylis found. Dr. Michael Forstner concluded the animal was a coyote with a disease called mange. Mange had caused the animal's hair to fall out in clumps. A second DNA test revealed the creature was a coyote mixed with a Mexican wolf. Phylis believes the chupacabra is actually a coyote mixed with some kind of wolf. Could this mysterious animal be the same type of creature that Madelyne Tolentino saw in Puerto Rico?

GLOSSARY

altitude sickness (AL-tuh-tood SIK-niss)—a condition that occurs when a person is high above sea level and the body does not get enough oxygen

ancestor (AN-ses-tuhr)—a member of a person's family who lived a long time ago

cryptid (KRIP-tihd)—a creature whose existence has not been proven by science

fault (FAWLT)—a crack in the earth where two plates meet; earthquakes often occur along faults

geologist (jee-AHL-uh-jist)—someone who studies minerals, rocks, and soil

mange (MAYNJ)—a skin disease that can cause hair loss in animals

skeptic (SKEP-tik)—someone who doubts or questions beliefs held by others

READ MORE

Colson, Mary. *Bigfoot and the Yeti.* Solving Mysteries with Science. Chicago: Raintree, 2014.

Marx, Mandy R. *Great Vampire Legends.* Vampires, Mankato, Minn.: Capstone Press, 2011.

Yomtov, Nel. *Tracking Sea Monsters, Bigfoot, and Other Legendary Beasts.* Unexplained Phenomena. Mankato, Minn.: Capstone Press, 2011.

INTERNET SITES

FactHound offers a safe, fun way to find Internet sites related to this book. All sites on FactHound have been researched by our staff.

Here's all you do:

Visit *www.facthound.com*

Type in this code: 9781491402429

Super-cool stuff!

Check out projects, games and lots more at
www.capstonekids.com

INDEX